First published in United States 2024

Published by Pacific Publications LLC

PO Box 1366 Corvallis OR 97339

Copyright © 2024 by Saaya

Cover Design © Sofie Draheim and Sarah Fastenmeier

Internal Artwork © Sarah Fastenmeier

Edited by Ari Annachi



ISBN: 978-1-922936-90-5

# Of Wolf and Shadow

Saaya

This is merely the beginning.

The black wolf appears between the world of what is, and what could be.

The crossroads, the corridor of choices,

so many paths lay before us.

This book is dedicated to the spirit of the shadow wolf that has appeared time and

time again to guide me along the way.

This is for Cu Sidhe, for the great Fenrir,

for Romeo

Lucian

Sadie

This is my dedication for my shadows

Saaya and Ekko

For Buddy


And it is for you my pack, my lost boys, my forged family.

For Brandon

Illustration by Meraea Hennessey

Within this book you will find there is no order here.
Rules are broken, time periods crossed or ignored in the
same sentence, poor grammar, and no
fixed/uniform/concise voice. There are many voices, tones,
styles, ages, expressions, perspectives— different rhymes,
different reasons.

The entirety of this work isn't meant to fit in any one
genre or label. It is my desire that there is at least one
piece of writing within these pages that may reach out
and offer you a hand. If only one, then I have done what
I came here to do. This book is for the non-conforming,
the chaotic, the emotional, the queer, the connected,
disconnected, desperate, hopeful, creative, and anyone
else just looking to be seen in some way. Many won't like
the utter nonsense they may find in this little genre
rebelling tome, but that is okay, there is space here for
you too.

Welcome to the Shadows

I write as "I" so that these stories may be for anyone who
resonates. These odes are for any– any shifter, dreamer,
creature, any person who sees themselves among them.
This is a respite, a home for who need it.
There is safety to be found, validation to be felt, and
strength to be seen between these pages.
Come as you are and stay as long as you need.

The dark half of the year always brings about
more thoughts and dreams of shape shifting.
There is a rich magic felt in the fall and winter
months. It is bittersweet as Imbolc passes and
the Cailleach hands over the year to Brigid,
taking us into the light half. Into the sun kissed
and blooming days.

Out of the sea and melting ice we came.

Everything is born out of water.

Even time is no match for the ice,

All is preserved within its frozen

embrace.

Water is the memory, the ancient mind.

It is alive and breathing into all things,

Connecting us with a forgotten past,

an unseen present,

and unknown future.

Wolf asked the humans,

"When you go to the trail, do you touch the trees? Do you know their names?

When you walk on the path so many have walked before you, do you feel the earth under your feet? The dirt, roots, the memories? Can you read the stories in a weavers web and interpret the songs of the winged? Do you remember your home? Or do you just push by it all for what it does for you, for the thrill of what you call adventure...

Do you know the elders whose saplings cover your forests, and the wisdom of a centuries old stream? Do you know me when you see me, do you know that we are the same? I am sibling to you, as you are sibling to me. It is time to return now to the great family we are all a part of.

My kin, it is time to remember..."

We did not come here to be teachers,

we came here to listen,

to learn.

To be the students of the world.

What wisdom could we give a 15,000 year old River?

What does Salamander or Squirrel need to learn from us about

surviving? It is Beaver who taught us to build shelter,

Wolf who taught us to live in community and work together to hunt,

to succeed.

What great knowledge could I teach a century old Tree?

Our feet have roots that seep so deep

into the dew moistened earth

with every step

we connect

not to hold to one place or time

but to rejoin the communal land map of those who

walked before

of those who rest

and those who now rise

# The Death Dealer

Rest now my brother, my sister,

for I will carry your strength and legacy in my being.

You will be remembered for all time as the earth will hold your bones

and mine together. Your blood passing from vein to teeth is sacred and I

shall honor you all my days by living well. Rest now, your pain and

struggle at last over, a beautiful beyond awaits until your time to emerge

anew.

Every spring the wolf offers up their warm winters' coat to the

land in thanks for its protection and survival through another cold

season.

This offering provides nesting materials for all kinds of creatures

and returns minerals to the ground.

Just as the wolf offers up a piece of themselves in thanks,

so too must we.

The welcoming of spring.

The wolf gives that which has sustained it through unrelenting

extremes and in return is gifted with new life. All is reciprocal.

Cyclical

Connected

Nothing is of waste or lacks purpose.

As I walk among volcanic
rock and Sagebrush,
following the Foxglove trail,
I see the land as it once was.
When feathered and furred rested
and played under White Oak.
I see the land as it once was,
unencumbered by man.

I want to jump off the towering rock holding your hand,

into the ocean and disappear beneath the waves

We will sing with sea giants and rest in the silent dark tides for a

time

But we shall not perish

We will return when trees and roots have reclaimed cities,

and the world is wild and full of magic as it once was

As it forever shall be

Wild lupine blooms along the edges of my spine

As wolves roam the forests

of my ever-restless mind

# The Guardian Promise

Listen closely little ones,

You are made of all those who came before you

You are their legacy

An archive of their stories rests within your blood and bone

Their triumphs, failures, strengths, mistakes

The wisdom of their experiences is their gift to you

Grow in the power of that knowing

Walk boldly in this world, for you are the future

And should you ever stumble, or find yourself with enemies,

know that one of us will be there to stand beside you

Remember,

we are always watching over you,

as you have watched over us

A bond sealed at the dawn of time

She read stories about the ancient people and wolves
that forged our future. Wolf and Human companions
destined to remind the others of our oneness.
She saw herself in these stories.
For no fire in her had ever burned more fiercely.
She would live and breathe and die for the wolves.
For our kin and their ancestors. If purpose is what it's
to be called.
The willingness to sacrifice even at the cost to one's
own desires.
The colonized mind wants to kill the wolf or to wear
the wolf mask in order to hide behind an imagined
sense of power. But they only risk within the bounds
that keep them safe.
The moment it no longer serves their selfish desires,
the wolf is abandoned or again cast away.
It was the shades that called her their own and showed
her she was meant for more than playing by man-made
rules. She would hurt, and she would struggle. She
would be a shadow, an outcast, but she would never
let them forget what we are.

The wolves kept their promise to watch over the humans.

It was through their connection with women, that we never forgot them.

We protect our families as they taught us, we see them in ourselves, and when the wolf comes howling, the wild inside us answers.

For we too are animal, are element, are nature.

All the damage humans have done, they have stayed to remind us of our way. Many have forgotten, many believe the old lies of those in power to keep us apart.

But anywhere there are wild women, whispers of rebellion, multi-species gatherings, or interdependent connection, you will find the wolves.

We are the way back to the mothers, we bare the

wellspring of life within our womb, and the wisdom of our people in our

bones. It is through our sacred companionship with our canine kin, and all of

our relations that heals. Women and wolves have long shared a similar fate, a

history marked in blood and pain yet carry a tending and nourishing medicine.

An oath and story long left to the shadows, forgotten or spoken over for

centuries. It is our time to reach back through the web of ages and reclaim our

tales and tails.

To walk in the old way, to pave the new.

Our Grandmothers do not always have smiling

wrinkled faces and warm gentle hands. Sometimes

they have broken fangs and ancient sorrow filled

eyes. Sometimes their white hair is stained with

aged iron and endings.

The wise one paused with labored breath.

Using the last of her strength to seal our fate with her final words.

"Just as the wolves have found the two of you. We become the watchers, the bridge between, and it is your turn now. The Wardens will try to trap you, control you, turn you on each other, exile you, and even slay you. They will weave stories of fear, betrayal, and hatred around you. But this will not stop you. Whatever happens now, whatever the future holds, this will remain. The pull towards one another will return in all of your lifetimes. For it is you, them, us, that will keep the balance and guide our kinds back to this sacred place.

To the root of all."

-An Ode to Promise of the Wolves

No matter the form that you take, I will know you

My soul will find you in all of our lifetimes

I will protect you, defend you

I will breathe for you

I will fight the battles you cannot win alone

I will stand for you when all others have forgotten

your wisdom

I will show them your ways by the path you have lain before us

Reaching through time to remind them who it was that walked

this earth first

Who it is that has adapted, evolved, survived for millennia

I will be your voice, your armor,

the thing that stands between you and oblivion

And we will let them know

we will not go quietly,

we will not be erased. . .

Illustration: Jade/ Kaaena

In appetite I am Raven, scavenger of flesh,

lover of gifts, provoking in play.

In walk I am branched antlers and warm breath, forest wanderer

and moss layer, stomped earth to protect heart and home.

In passion I am Wolf, hungering hunter, devourer,

remembered moon song, and thirst for the blood of creation.

In life I am Changeling, strangered enigma,

oscillating shifter of pleasure and pain, belonging and outcast.

In rest I am bark skinned and rooted, breathing and receiving.

In feeling I am Storm and Sea, alluring waters,

mysteriously hidden depths, and violent tempests.

I am the mergence of oppositions.

Where the North meets the South.

Where East embraces West, while Sun and Moon kiss in the twilight

sky.

We are the entangled limbs of cedar and fir,

where wolf and reindeer run as one.

We are the coming together of what was believed to never be.

You are walking rebellion, resistance.

I am the thinning veil between worlds, the place beyond the void.

Together we hold a surging revolution that will give birth to a new

age.

Sometimes it felt unbearable to be human…

Running on awkward legs too slow, with lungs that give out long

before the desire to cease ever arises. A silent torment when the entirety

of my body can so easily remember what it was to run with wolves.

On four paws, lungs full without straining, strong lean limbs to carry me

swift and far with little effort.

I feel a great joy and a great sadness running beside my canine

companion. I can feel his every muscle as if they were my own, yet I am

so limited. It is the same when I see the flight of Raven or Hawk. I can

feel wind under spread feathers lifting up, soaring. As if my soul

remembers a time when I could. Sometimes being human feels like

punishment.

We forget who we are, what we are, what we are a part of. We forget

we are animal and how to be animal. How to be one with water and

earth. We have ears drowning in deafening noise and noses poisoned

with synthetic perfumes.

Does Raven remember what it's like to howl or to have hands?

Does Bear remember being Salmon or Stream?

Maybe that is the gift of these bodies, to feel deeply and connect with the

others in a way only we can. To expand and embrace,

instead of drown out.

Maybe the beauty of being human is that both the gift and the

punishment are truth.

The seasoned ones never could get me to learn to human quite right. And

even less so to be proper as they called it.

I was a hunched little creaturling, curled with knees to chest.

Hiding in shadows, creeping around corners, and perched up in high

places. Crouching on counters, chairs, rooftops. Knots never left my hair,

and I hated the feel of socks and shoes.

I wanted to feel it all.

It felt so strange and difficult to move elegantly or walk gracefully like

some of the others could. My human keepers complained how I ruined

my arms and legs with scars from playing too hard, and I

never could work out why bleeding and scabs were "ugly".

Why they weren't just as perfect as unblemished skin. I preferred the

proof of living.

Untouched skin meant too sheltered, too many rules, restrictions. Being

too clean, too straight, too mannered meant being caged.

Whatever for would someone want to be a flightless bird?

Cuts and bruises meant to me that I was strong, adventurous, brave. A

child always hearing they're too big, too much, too loud changes to adapt.

But then they will complain with you're too quiet, too avoidant of their

company,

too secretive. I was too much a boy, too much a girl, but not enough to be a

boy, and not enough to be a girl. Now they see nothing of me. Not even

whispers of my stories.

You see that's what happens when you try to domesticate the wild. They will

make their escape no matter the cost and they will be gone.

For good.

They will be free.

My handwriting is messier than usual

and the unfinished letters are relatable to the gap between my thoughts.

Anxiety, overstimulation, a violent cyclone underneath my skin. It is the soon to be erupting volcano. My body wishes to dispense of this festering duress, but the building crescendo seems as though it will swallow me whole. As though bones will fragment and rupture, and my form will cease to exist. I wonder amidst such intense discomfort if this is what shape-shifting feels like. When they hold the wolf for too long attempting to be tame.

Masking is just that isn't it?

My experience as an autistic being places us closer to the wild nature. How cruel it was to give it a name that causes shame, rejection.

A disorder?

How cruel they are to taint its true nature.

Wild, adapting, inherent.

Animals shake, sing, roar, and stim.

They play and move energy as they experience it. My struggle is only due to the way society made me fear how it looks when my body contorts out of my control in an effort to return to some semblance of balance, peace. But I know surrender is the only way. Fighting the roaring tide within me only quickens the drowning. I wish physically changing shape was an option when these spells come. Evanescing into the formless would bring insurmountable and desperately needed relief.

To have no vessel, no flesh for a while.

To be wind rustling through the tops of trees,

what bliss that seems.

I love this body, this mind.

But what if I could dissolve like a snowflake into a river.

What if I could be the fog of a

wolf's breath or the sound of an avalanche.

Free from form, constrictions, from weight.

Free from pain.

I think I would join the north wind and ride to the night sky to dance with my ancestors for a time in the foxfire.

Artwork by Martith

There are words that once spoken, move mountains inside others.
That make possible dreams only previously dared to be whispered. At
the lowest and darkest spaces, it was the wisdom of wolves, and
words of women that were the beacon and gentle guiding hands.
Some are born by a blazing sun and conviction for a path they know
belongs to them, and no fear in claiming it.

Like a compass ever pointing North, they know their way. Others of
us were born under no such sun to guide us forward. Instead only the
company of shadows through misty lands, with the echos of
daydreams. Searching for this directional force known as purpose. But
looking outside is how we lose our way, when the answers lie within
those dark forests we've spent our whole lives trying to leave,
forgetting it is our home. It is our way. To live by the moon, to run, to
howl, to hunt, to take up space in this world in ways only we can.

I'm never going to want to smile for men

I want to smile for bats swooping in the twilight sky

For lightning veins reaching across purple night

My smile is for boars' war cry, territorial bumble bees, and foraging bears

The boisterous rumble arising from my throat is

for wolves

I share soft laughter with rats scurrying the rooftop, opossums in my garden,

and moths that kiss my shoulders

I beam for arachnids weaving multipurpose geometrical masterpieces

and coyote chaos after dark

The curve of my lips is my thank you to slithering serpentine friendships and

amphibious chorus

I will never want to smile for men

who feel it owed and fear everything the dark touches

My laughter, my joy, is for the forgotten,

the unknown, the outcasts,

for the shadows

Why should I be concerned what humans
think of me?
I care what the forest thinks of me.
I want Hawthorne to know my heart and
swallows to dance in fondness when they
hear my name.
I want to be welcomed by bees and
embraced by River.
Smiled upon by elder Sun.
Remembered as the wayward child who
found their way home.

Most days

I do not identify as woman, man,

outside the binary, or even human.

I identify with creature.

With chaos wrapped in skin.

Wind makes more sense to me.

Water.

Like I would evaporate into the air,

form an expansive cloud,

rage with thunder, strike lightning,

and arrange myself as rain to soak deeply into

the moist soft earth.

To nourish

and repeat.

It feels like words have left  me dry

Parched

Even the ideas feel famine

Drought of inspiration

I wish the rains to come again and soak my soul with drops of

magic.

Not for myself, but as an offering I can give back.

And as I sit here the words begin to stir as I write.

I hear Boar's message break the silence.

He says write, do not stop,

this is why you're here.

Ignore the chatter.

You did not come to stifle yourself and lose sight in their

songs. Look only forward and move. Become inertia,

take a step,

walk,

run,

become wind.

Stomp earth,

and watch life spring forth from the underworld.

Be thunder upon dirt...

...Breath

Fill the space between your ribs with every detail.

And with these words the sky splits open pouring showers

upon inspirations return.

I can feel creation reawakening through every part of my

being.

Golden starlight brimming beneath every inch of my skin.

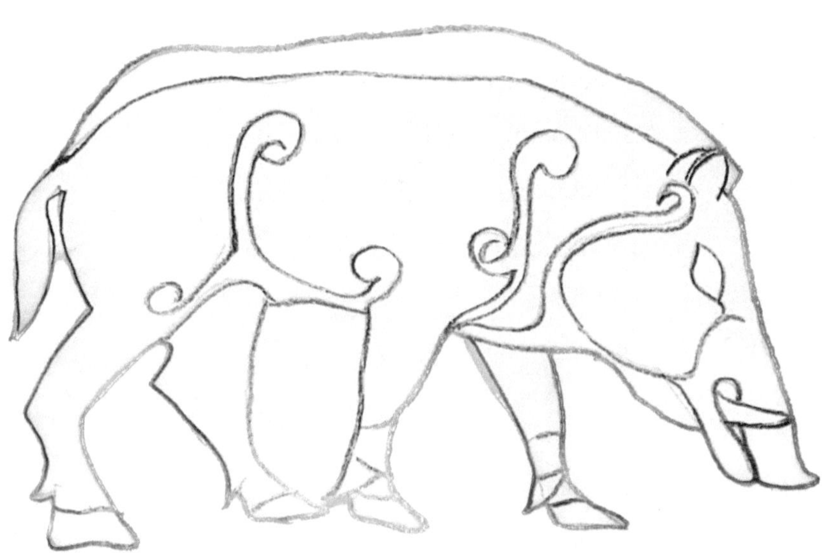

The pressure begins to release,

the stagnant muck begins to flow onward.

Dirty water running more clearly by the page.

I want to keep coming here. Returning to the magic of ink and trees.

My greatest sanctuaries and reliefs in times I cannot escape.

Wise barked giants, aged tomes,

and these pages.

In the secret world of the writer, there lies a tree spirit

who is hearing and holding all that is raw and real.

Spilled across page after page.

A spirit sitting quietly with me as I feel,

as I ache, express, grieve, and release.

Thank you to the elder holding these words.

I wonder if I had an ancestor who loved to write

and tell stories, or perhaps one who desired to but

couldn't.

Seems there could be many, being descendent of

those whose way of life

centered around storytelling.

As I come to the sacredness of this form of love,

my own ailments dissipate between the lines on

the page.

The place where my body, mind, and soul unify in

relieved thanks.

May these ancestors feel and at last be fulfilled.

*Remember that you are more than yourself.*

*There are parts of you that ache to paint, to*

*dance, to sing, to write, bake, build,*

*to create.*

*Parts that are shared with those of your lineage*

*that maybe never had the chance to pursue.*

*So create*

*for yourself, for your ancestors whom you carry*

*within, and for us. We are waiting to see what is*

*only authentically you.*

THIS IS THE NEXT STEP FOR MY JOURNEY.

TO ENTER THE VOID AND FIND WHAT AWAITS THERE.

MAYBE THERE IN THE NOTHING,

THE EVERYTHING,

THE WHALE SONG WILL FIND ME.

Descendant of salmon wisdom and holy flowing waters
Descendant of magic and smoke clouds' journey to a
wolf laden land
Descended from the ice and glacial teethed mountain
caves
From she who brings sorrow, child of the giants' forest
Raised by trolls, wolves, elfing elders, and spiraling
symbols

All around us the Earth sings her melody

Our ancestors heard and sang along

contributing to the Great Song

But we have forgotten our part and lost our way

It's time to listen and remember

The melody is within us

We are a part of it and it a part of us

A single note that when combined with the other voices of our world

becomes the beautiful Song of Life

It shows us how to flow with the seasons and cycles

I remember the song

I have returned

The corvids watch our movements as the
eyes of the ancestors
They remember and pass on our stories

His yellow eyes were
warmer than the sun
and just as bright
Photograph taken by Ashley Janssen

A treasure trove of glittering words sparkle in those eyes.

But for now, I think I'll keep our secrets.

To say Nature is merciless, is to not truly know her.

In the same ways others have found only destruction, death, loss, I have found her mercy in the balance between the hunter and the hunted. A cool water oasis in the scorching summer.

The wolf leader who has never lost a fight and never killed an opponent. But her greatest mercy has been in the way most animals have not exercised violence on our two-legged race, and that we have only survived as naked beasts because of this mercy. Her mercy can be found in the warmth of sunlight after a bitter dark winter, or in the rain during a time of drought.

She is always showing us the beauty of mercy, if we do not fail to look for it.

Glimmers from the dark-

Instead of glimmers like that of sunlight, cool

breeze, butterfly wings.

Glimmers from lightning and the crash of thunder.

A glimmer in a power outage, silence below the surface of the sea,

firelight.

What wondrous emotion a storm holds,

the predators' eyes that flicker in the night.

I followed the fading light into the land. For me there is no cure quite like this. Absolute silence as you rise above the clouds, lungs straining, heart pounding, muscles burning. The mind has no space, no volume to it here. You are reduced to body, soul, and will alone. All there is, is you and the ground beneath your feet as you convince yourself there is no other option but to press forward. I know this is why some of us have no choice but to come back to land or sea when all else seems to fail. It's not an escape....it's a return to the start. It's a stripping to the bones of who and what we are. We are nothing more or less than our truest selves in these moments…

There is not sacrifice, but an intimacy, an offering to life.

To offer one's exhalation and in return be bestowed

with vital breath. To offer decaying flesh to sweet decomposition

as fuel for regeneration of the land body.

We exist in reciprocation of one another.

What could be more intimate than a being breathing in your life

force and returning to you that of its own?

We become a part of each other. Much of life is like this.

No matter how you believe to be apart from it,

we are ever blissfully entangled.

We walked among the old ones and on the land of giants.

Wondering if they felt our presence as we feel theirs.

If they recognize us as their children returned home.

These are our parents, our elders, our people.

A sacred truth we would not forget in any of our lifetimes.

No more gods

Nearly two decades spent calling out to a silent voice beyond the sky, suffering, alone, in agony.

Begging and pleading for the mercy that was so often told this all mighty one would bestow. It was not quite like being ignored, as it was there was no mighty "one" there listening at all. It was when I let the poison I had been spoon fed dissipate, that I heard all the voices around me. The droplets of dew on flowers' edge, snowflakes in my lashes, the gentle wind that ushers in spring, crow wings, butterfly kisses, the rustle of leaves. I had never been alone. And never again would I be.

Photography of Lucien by Rachel Lauren

Artwork by Sarah Fastenmeier

When I called out to a god
it was the ancients who answered
The horned and fanged
leather winged and siren voiced in the night
Those of twisted roots and thorny veins
with hoof and claw to aid them
It was the mountain who spoke my name
The forest warden took me in,
and the bone gatherer taught me
the way of stories

I went to the forest and fell to my knees in anguish.

I have never been more held than in hunter shaded cathedrals.

The holiest places I've ever

beheld sound of deafening

silences, bloodstained choruses,

and roaring riptides. The only god

I know is the one I'm standing on

and with her I am never without.

Mycelium tendrils softly seep into temples, and I hear the voices of a thousand

forests. These are the ancient gods of the underworld.

What place is there for fear in such beauty, such union.

Emerald Mosses make the slow waltz across fading flesh, and cradles weary

bones deep into the soil bed. A gentle embrace as the body's biome gives way to

moisture laden landscape.

I belong to the undergrowth, and I surrender to the serenity of this deep slumber.

Illustration by Keri Duckworth

In desperate moments,

fall against the moss beds in serene surrender.

Be swallowed up in the great mothers' arms,

and ease into her beating heart.

Does the forest rejoice when we die?

For she knows we are returning to her. Her wisdom tells of our pain's final

hours with not left to fear, for she will gently hold our bodies as we return to her

earthly womb.

Our lives given and new life begins.

Does the forest see our end as a home coming?

A celebration awaits us.

NO FOREST
BELONGS
TO MAN.
Illustration by Ludvig Levin

Why does walking by the chopped up fallen bodies of our rooted

relations not horrify so many of us the way a battlefield does?

The mass destruction of our bark skinned elders haunts me no

differently than a warzone. The forest gives us the very air we breathe

and yet we so easily commit the most shameful of crimes.

The same brutality thrashed upon all of creation, that only the

primordial elements can cease.

It is past time we allow the ghosts of our own making to haunt us into

transformation.

We can no longer settle for less.

We are now in the time of the Great Remembering.

Imagine if you will, running through a giant's forest.

Where everything is alive not just by breathing, but moving, thrashing, leaping, twirling, gnawing, and so much larger than your cities. Towers become moving titans, planes are hungry pterodactyls, and trains are serpents searching for a meal. In this world being quick would be an ally. For if you're too slow you will be stepped on, captured, crushed, eaten. Now, imagine your purpose is to help the small place you live thrive. You remove the pests that plague tree bark and fox skin. All the while dressing any place you make home with glistening auric tapestries....

So next time you see spider or small creature racing towards you, imagine fleeing from a giant beast towards a tree, but the tree becomes a troll trying to squash you simply for fleeing its way.

This is the big world of small beings.

As the local garter slips through my fingers rapidly into the brush, do they think they have narrowly just escaped death?

You were never in danger from me little one,

but I wonder how often is this the happenings of other paths we may cross.

The larger more dangerous kind that leave us thinking-

today I was lucky.

But in truth we were never in danger to begin with.

Life feels unreal, otherworldly in the presence of almighty landscapes. Perhaps that feeling is because we are so encoded by the programming of society, that we no longer get to see how beautiful this planet really is.

Maybe it's not otherworldly at all.

As humans we have been intentionally ripped from our ancestral and transformational entanglement with the cosmic fabric of existence. We look beyond the stars for answers that are right under our feet. We live with our head in cyberspatial clouds, instead of being present on the ground, present with each other. There is no need to escape to some far off place to experience wonder. Wonder is just beyond the technological perception. There is magic to be found in every part of this terrestrial body we inhabit.

Go out. Find it.

Pull the plug and disengage from the systems designed to keep you in line, to keep you complacent in your own suffering until the day you die. Make it your mission to reconnect back into the world and hold fast to this ancient and sacred tether.

Their credit cards, their
crypto, their assets and dollar
bills mean nothing beyond their
doors, beyond the cityscapes and
buzzing electrical currents.
What happens when the lights go
off?
When all the noise of progress
stops?
Will their plastic squares, dead
phones, and frozen bank accounts
feed them?
Nurture their bodies and quench
their thirst?
Will their money buy them
survival?

INEVITABLY IT ALL MUST END.

WHAT RISES MUST FALL.

IT'S UP TO US WHAT COMES NEXT...

FREEDOM

Free are those who awaken in the black of night, or the dawn of

morning and exhale from the spirit. Those who cradle the deep

knowing that there is nowhere one begins and the other ends,

we are all in flux, growing, reverberating

off each other's cells in infinite intermingling existence.

Freedom lives in those who's very life breath is an act of rebellion.

For to be of the spirit, one's true expression,

is to break through every chain, every binding, tower, or wall meant to

keep order.

Freedom is in the folds of chaos.

Don't listen when they call you destroyer of peace

Disturbance seeker

When their order is built on denial,

on lies

Your chaos is beautiful in the way it crumbles falsehoods exposing truth

Photograph by Cyrena Rose

It was never the beasts who were the monsters of the
story

Creatures who have dwelled and protected their lands

for eons just to have some human decide in a matter of

moments that they must be evil

No longer did fair maidens fear the woods or believe the twisted tales of creatures dwelling there. Spun to keep them contented to a meager and dutiful living, away from wandering and the magic of living a life all their own. The women had found their way to the wolves again, and what is there to fear when the monster of the story greets you as welcome friend.

GROWING UP IS REALIZING MOST OF THE VILLAINS OF
OUR CHILDHOOD STORIES WEREN'T VILLAINS AT ALL.
THEY WERE RIGHTFULLY ANGRY, REBELLIOUS, AND
FIGHTING FOR CHANGE THEY BELIEVED IN, OR THEY ARE
THE PRODUCT OF THE CRUELTIES AND INJUSTICES OF
SOCIETY. WE ARE RAISED TO THINK THESE BEINGS OF
CHANGE ARE TO BE REJECTED AND CAST OUT.
HOW DARE THEY FEEL REBELLIOUS TO ACTIONS THAT
CAUSED THEM OR OTHERS TO SUFFER.
HOW DARE THEY WISH TO TAKE HOLD AND MOLD A
BETTER FUTURE.

They set our grandmothers ablaze.

Our mothers turned into betrayers and enslaved.

Now a whole generation of dragon raised girls emerge

out of the inferno they once used to erase.

You cannot give fire to rage.

You simply gave fuel to the flame....

I am volcanic ash,

singeing breath from lungs

I am eruptive rage, cataclysmic fire

I am the end of all things

Scorched rock and boiling ocean

There are no senses beyond my grasp

I leave you burned a sunder

What do men know of true power?

Of dragon fire

Of wolf fury

Of woman's wrath

# DRAGON'S FIRE

There is a rage crawling up my bones, burning in my lungs and throat.

Like dragon's fire.

Rage.

Blood family feels like a curse to some of us. A brand we take scorching steel to carve out. We cauterize the putrid seeping wound. Rage is holy fire to cleanse such malignant coagulation. The blood of the covenant, the chosen, far stronger than the curdled water of an abandoned womb.

## RAGE.

Seeing the repeat of our childhood in the little faces of those new to emerge, as they turn to violence and self-blame.

Rage, dragon fire.

Wanting to burn it all.

Justice for a younger self. Justice for the pain and suffering.

Justice is dragon fire,

but so is agony...

And I'm overflowing.

My palms and marrow burn.

So much volcanic heat rising under my skin.

I've held it for too long on my own.

Rage is held sacred by the people

One's village

Agony is not meant to be cradled alone

But in the arms of solidarity

Burning our women, our medicine, our friends didn't quite have
the effect you wanted, did it?
Instead of extinguishing that which you feared,
dragons rose up out of the ashes.
And you surmised sending knights to slay them would be
remedy enough.
Ever wonder why dragons always take the maidens of the story?
Why they hoard the treasure?
We've been here before haven't we?
What would happen if a dragon raised girl made it to
womanhood? With ferocity, and wealth,
and a lack of ego driven heroes to stop her?
Ah yes, there's the answer isn't it....

NO MORE WILL WE BE THE SACRIFICE.
NO MORE WILL WE DIE FOR THE CAUSES OF MEN OR
GODS.
YOU WILL NOT TAKE ANY MORE OF OUR SISTERS,
MOTHERS, DAUGHTERS, NO MORE OF OUR WOMEN.
AND WE WILL NO LONGER BELIEVE THE LIES THAT
OUR VALUE COMES IN HOW MUCH WE ARE WILLING
TO SACRIFICE.

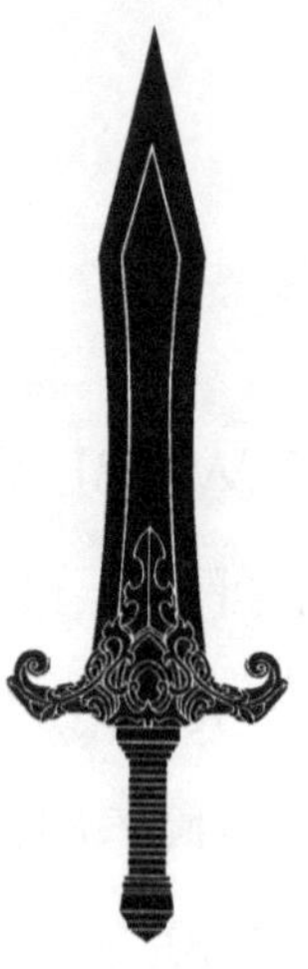

But fury can be molded into passion.

If there are no stories,

we will write them.

If there are no tales of our kind,

of those like you, like me, like us,

we will tell them.

We will speak,

we will write,

we will carve and sing and thread together the tapestry

of our likeness.

We will not be erased.

We will not fall silent.

We will not be unknown to the future.

The dichotomy of being in these bodies is this
We may carry peace and love and hope gently in one
hand
While we claw and bite and fight for it with blood or
steel in the other
We may nourish and protect
As we enact retribution

We think by defining something, we've come to
understand it.
But I would argue the moment we define
something; we lose the chance of understanding
and have only placed limits on how it can be known.

Perhaps I am the nameless

I have been searching so long for a name that feels like my own

None feel like home reverberating from the throats of caves

or from my own lips

None have yet to summon my soul

Perhaps I am the unnamed

For how does a deviant settle on a singular calling?

Perhaps I am of many names, an illusionary spirit

I am perceived through a thousand different lenses by that which I am

called upon

An Enigma

for no such name exists that can contain the essence

of those who are chaos to some, and

serenity to others

When they ask me how I identify, I tell them I don't.

My identity is the wind blowing through ancient Hawthorn branches,

the forming of snow crystals, the churning tide, and the echos of

bioluminescent caverns. My sexuality is the eruption of volcano, the

cooling rain fall, it is Snake shedding her skin, and Wolf during the hunt.

Do not ask me to check boxes with such narrow ideas that could not

begin to fathom a drop in the sea of what it is to be alive.

Identities are for other people.

To remind themselves who you are, who they are.

For the chaos born, those who know that we are ever changing, we have

no use for being organized, confined.

I am all that you see,

and I am nothing.

From the OtherSide


Humans... sometimes so strange.

They center so much around names.

What to call things, call each other in order to recognize anything outside of

themselves.

Do they not know each other by their essence?

Will they not know me if they do not have something to call me?

Will they not know themselves?

I wonder what is this fascination with names,

and it's purpose in this world we share.

There are fairytales happening all around you every day

if you have the eyes to see. Magical and fantastical characters living among

you in plain sight. That old woman with the wide brimmed hat and no teeth

picking berries while talking to the trees. The loner with the wolf looking dog

walking by a little boy who points and asks his parents if werewolves are real,

all while not taking his eyes off them.

The child that's a naturally gifted swimmer whose

parents can never seem to get them out of the water.

The teenage musical prodigy or the

one who is

always

followed by butterflies.

These are the hearts of your stories.

They were real…. All of them.

All the stories, the poems, the tales of beings from another realm. They are here still. What makes a historical story more or less true than the 1,000-year-old folk tale of the woman who rose out of the sea in sealskin to see her lover every seven years?

Or the forest warden who was loved by a village boy. There are endless stories of crossings between our worlds as friend, as lover or companion, as apprentice. Just as we know there were other kinds of humans in our history, and we are the walking mixture of those people, so too are there living descendants of the selkie, the trolls' children, the changelings, the wolf walkers. Perhaps that is why some of us feel we do not belong here, do not understand or feel understood amongst humankind. Why some of us spend our whole lives dreaming under stars and complete in unwanting for that which man created.

I hear desert

Feel her pulling

The secret yet to be found

Something is watching, waiting

The feeling as though just at the edge of discovery,

dragging fingertips over ridged xanthous towers

My veins run dry and I fall to the sand again

Sandstone saffron

I'm lost in the elements again

I feel my body crack like fire

and I'm off on the wind

Fanning my desire

I'm ready to swim

I'm pushing up through the dirt reaching for sunlight

The creeper crawling the tree

high up in the moonlight

Silver threads glistening in the morning dew

Stardust gathering around the moon

The Raven caws,
bringing on their wings the gentle east winds.
Carrying messages of change,
softening my stiff aching muscles.
Raven circles back,
beckoning me to follow.
This way they say,
to the answer of that which you seek.

Algiz, you've been calling me.

Quietly and patiently, you needn't make yourself known like so many

others. Your appearance in the distance a gentle breeze, a reminder. You

are never far. You have always been here, as you always will be.

Great horned one.

You feel as an old friend welcoming me home.

I soften under your gaze.

The strangulation of my

overworked human form

eases off my frame, and I am free

to join you in your forests.

I feel as though I am entering a great learning.

Without a sound you have much to say

and paths to show me. I have longed for

this meeting, but did not know it was you

I wished to see.

When writing calls, a writer appears.
I can feel that glittering magic stirring once again
beneath the surface.
The hairs on my arms rise up like spider legs.
Summer is coming to a close.
Soon my spirit will emerge from bone and ash and
scrape claw upon the dirt.
Howling in sweet agony as I don true form at last..
The echos of extinct, departed, lost, extinguished,
and newly birthed stories grow louder, swirling about
the caverns of my mind.
Ready at any moment to erupt from throat or
fingertip.

With autumn's arrival comes the time of the deep magic. The veil thins
and abundant creations flow to our side of the realm. The equinox is
when I exchange my once
human flesh in return to four weathered paws and descend into the dark.
My wild turned loose where it may run and play and rest as it sees fit.
Where pretense and cordiality are no longer required. I am raw here.
Fresh out of the steaming heap of my summer form. Cozied up in my
furs, tail, and fangs, I am home.
This is the time of beasts, magic, and wonder. I will run with the reindeer
again for another season. I will roam moss filled forests with the
drumming of hooved mystics and whispers of the ancients.

All that lies dormant in the spring and summer
months will awaken in ancestral blood.
The wind has begun to bring to me soft
echos to come. The worlds are merging,
and I am dripping in etheric essence.

Child of wind and water.

Forged by sea and storm, I crawled out of an ocean wave that crashed amidst blackened stone talons. Sculpted by ghostly mist laden isles, and the glacial fangs of dark mountains. I sprang forth from a she-wolf's blood-stained ballad, for she is my mother.

Not I as in me, I as the embodied journey of my lineages.

This is a tale of She.

Origin.

She lives within the raging storm of my eyes.

She awakens through the dark portals their swirling tidepools hold. She is the rhythmic thunder drumming behind my marrowed shield, and fleshed armor.

Soon I will follow the reindeer trod across glacial deserts, beyond

the frost bitten mists in the realm of twilight.

The ravens have already taken to the skies above the herd, and it

is time for the pack to follow.

Elun is the origin mother, the pathway finder, and to survive in

the far north we have followed her for eons.

The one who once nourished the first giant and revived beast

from frozen sleep. The drumming of her hooves summon our

beating hearts to her call.

I have a grandmother who is reindeer.

Horns like branches and seeping with magic.

Knower and holder of ways.

She came to me first in images and dream. She told me although I did not remember her name, she was with me.

The winter has been bitter and harsh white light like the snows of the far north. She tells me to keep going. Find warmth within herd and self within midnight wolf song.

A wolf's howl does not get lost in the sea of the pack.

Each song is unique, precious, and needed.

Irish Elk ancestor tells me to be strong, to not be ashamed of who I am. If I fall, all I must do is hold on and antlers will raise me back to my feet. Furred nose will gently nudge me on.

Cervid is mighty spirit.

She says walk with me, and you will never be lost.

For you are a child of the ways...

Illustration by Hester Aspland

# Vaihtaja

There was a girl who spoke to the trees and slept with the wolves.

Her eyes held stormy tides and the pierce of lightning. Upon winter, mist seeped from her pores as she slipped away from her human form, her bones sinking down into the deep moss to lie in rest until spring. She shifted on the north wind into the silent fall of snow. She was everywhere, and no where all the same. You could find her in the steam rolling from the Red Stag's breath as he bellows to the others, in the warm blood of Wolverine as she caches meat from carrion. Whispers of her trickled down the nearly frozen falls, and you could hear her in the cracking of ice. Her sole trait left unchanging, is her home amongst the wolves. If all other signs alluded the senses, you were sure to catch her in frosted dew drops on greyed or blacked wolf back.

On the echoing howls of a successful hunt.

There she would always be found.

There are wolves who walk among you in the bodies of women.

And there are women who roam the wilds on four legs with blood

stained teeth and bushy tails.

But whether in wolf skin or flesh of a human

The wolf, the woman, and the wild remain.

I sang my heart over a pile of old bones.

And called to me flesh made of numerous celestial bodies.

The birth of a cosmic singularity.

Photograph by Rachel Lauren

Sometimes it becomes too tiresome to try

to hide the hollow of my spine

The spiders in my hair or the echo of an ancient forest from my voice

Times have changed, and I am but a shade of the ancient being I once was

Feared, honored, counseled

No longer do they come to the forest with offerings

No longer do they ask permission

The humans have forgotten their place in the wider world beyond their perception

The only thing time has left unaltered is men's greed…

They still come in hopes of capturing the beautiful maiden,

forgetting that I am just as terrifying and merciless, as I am generous

And I do not forgive those who have harmed my beloved woods, my home

The great mountains may be sleeping, the swamps may have fallen quiet, and we may be

but whispers in your time

But do not forget,

we are here and we are watching

The stirring has begun

Soon I will no longer hide my tail

The resting giants will wake, the wolves will rise

And we will take back the world we left to you

Balance is the absolute law and you cannot continue to take from that

which you do not give in return

Artwork by Bex Dartnall

Artwork by Ludvig Lavin

How long had it been,

that we moved silently in the world behind the Féth fíada?

How long have we lived watching from the otherside?

Once, Éire was known as Wolf Land,

but when the priests found their way across Eileanan Bhreatainn, our

kind were hunted down and destroyed. Those that remained retreated

and have been living among the Sidhe. But our time is nearing.

The time of the wolf's return.

Centuries have passed and the human world has changed. More are

remembering, more are standing against that which tried to erase us. They

are letting go of the ways brought by those who seek only to control.

Keep your eyes on the fog ridden horizon, for someday soon, we will

emerge from the mists once more....

Illustration by Shannon Cornell

There are stories of a phantom hound that
comes to lead you to a crossroad
They say he is the gatekeeper and guide to the Otherworld
Cú Sídhe was what they called him in one lifetime
But he has been my friend for many
Our stories have been
written throughout the ages
It's time we write one more
Illustration by Martich

Cú Sidhe

I heard his eerie howl…That black spectral hound from beyond the veil. He's waiting for me, deep in the ancient forest where the many paths meet. As the embers of my hearth fire crackle and spark in their last efforts to burn, I too cling to the fading warmth and comforts of this too small and weathered dwelling. For I know my time has come. The winds howl, beckoning at my crooked, battered door and a shiver runs the length of my spine. I feel his patient burning eyes. I know them well. We have danced together through our many lifetimes. And I know like my own shadow, there is no escape to this red stringed fate. He waits for now, though he is hungry. My dying fears and skins of past, his offerings. I take a last look about this place I've long outgrown. A final farewell to my ghosts as I feed the fire once more. In the growing darkness he waits……

the unbecoming has begun…

He came to me on the silent whispers of the winter winds.

He was of mists and shadows.

A melancholy dream of another life passed, haunting the corridors of

my memory. His spectral form roaming the landscapes of my heart,

but now he comes to call me home. To spirit me away at last, to the

place my soul shall run free from my many prisons once more.

Long have I waited....

"Won't you tell me a story?"


And he sang to me tales of great love and great sorrow.

And of how we came to be . . .

What use do I have of dreams?

When every morning my heavy lids rise to find home in your eyes.

When your thunderous song echos in my ears and drowns out the

chaos of my never silent mind. There is no dreamland as sweet as the

silence of these shared moments. If the dream is where we say goodbye,

I'd rather stay awake.

Have you ever looked in someone's eyes and felt your whole being come under their hold for a single moment? You're just loose, floating with no tether until they look into your eyes, and suddenly there is gravity.
Their heartbeat commands the wild in yours to come to peace.

The Shadow leads me to the place unseen

Elysium composed by my wildest dreams

Whispers beckon I go forth into the dark

And rest my bones within Járnvidr's heart

As I followed him through the gloaming realm

I realized this dark landscape was a respite for those

scourged by existence

A place of solace,

curative to the weary, downtrodden

spirits who wander herein

It was then I knew why he brought me here

To this place within the ethos of the soul

This was a journey of redemption

Of becoming…

Some stories feel
like home
Like another life,
like memories…

# SAAYA

Time and memory, such fickle creatures.

Some moments feel as fresh as the breath just taken,

others feel an eternity away, requiring more to reach back and summon to the surface.

It seems but a blink on the grand scale while looking back, but truly I have lived so many

lives in the era of you. I have gone through my darkest days transforming in the depths of

your shadowed presence, resurfacing changed in your wake. And I continue to live in this

flux and flow as we walk along the crossroad's edge.

It is easy to say we would die for a cause, a person we love.

It is an entirely different feat to say we would live for something.

To live through the horror, the pain, and to forge a path forward when it feels there is

nothing worth breathing for.

You gave it all meaning.

What I know for certain, I will never have enough time or enough memories with you.

I hope there is a lifetime where we never have to part,

my shadow..

On that day so many years ago the life I had known ended, and a new one began. A life full of dreams made real, adventure, metamorphosis, freedom of the truest form, the kind of suffering that cracks your very being open, and a love that has taken me to the very depths of my soul.

And this is only the beginning, the mere first chapters in a series of stories we have still yet to write. You have given me more and taken me farther than I ever imagined. You have shown me some journeys are meant only for those willing to leave the comfort of their cages, their illusions, and walk into the depths of the dark. To let go of constructed ideas in exchange for pure authentic presence.

You came and set the wild in me free.

Every time oblivion called my name,

you called it a little louder.

When my mind worked against me, dragging me into the abyss, you sent a howl ringing through my chest to remind my heart how to beat. And when I was gasping for air, drowning in a flood I thought would never end, you dried my eyes and offered the warmth of your fur, the slow steady rise and fall of your breath, and the rhythmic beat of your heart to show me I never have to face this alone. There are so many times my story would've ended without you. Chapters left unwritten, a plot twist left undiscovered, a happy ending that never had a chance to be read. Whenever I could not find a reason, I could look in your golden eyes and find a million why I should stay. Why there was no choice other than to keep going. Many people think the most epic love stories are romantic ones. I think we are living proof that's not always the case. For I have never loved anyone or anything with the depth of my soul, the way I love you. I would not stay fighting for this life for anyone but you. Because no one has ever seen all the ugliest parts of me the way you have and shown me I'm still worth loving. That I'm worth redeeming. And that even when it feels I have nothing left in me, I can look at you and see all the love that's never faltered.

They will sing tales of our ferality through their many lifetimes.

How it stirred them,

disturbing the long settled dust atop their forgotten dreams.

How it caused to question what they had dared not seek answered.

You and I will live on,

the untamable shadow lurking amongst their sinews.

Ever thrashing wild beneath their ribs,

with the promise to one day break free.

One day they all shall come,

calling upon us once again.

And one day, we too shall answer.

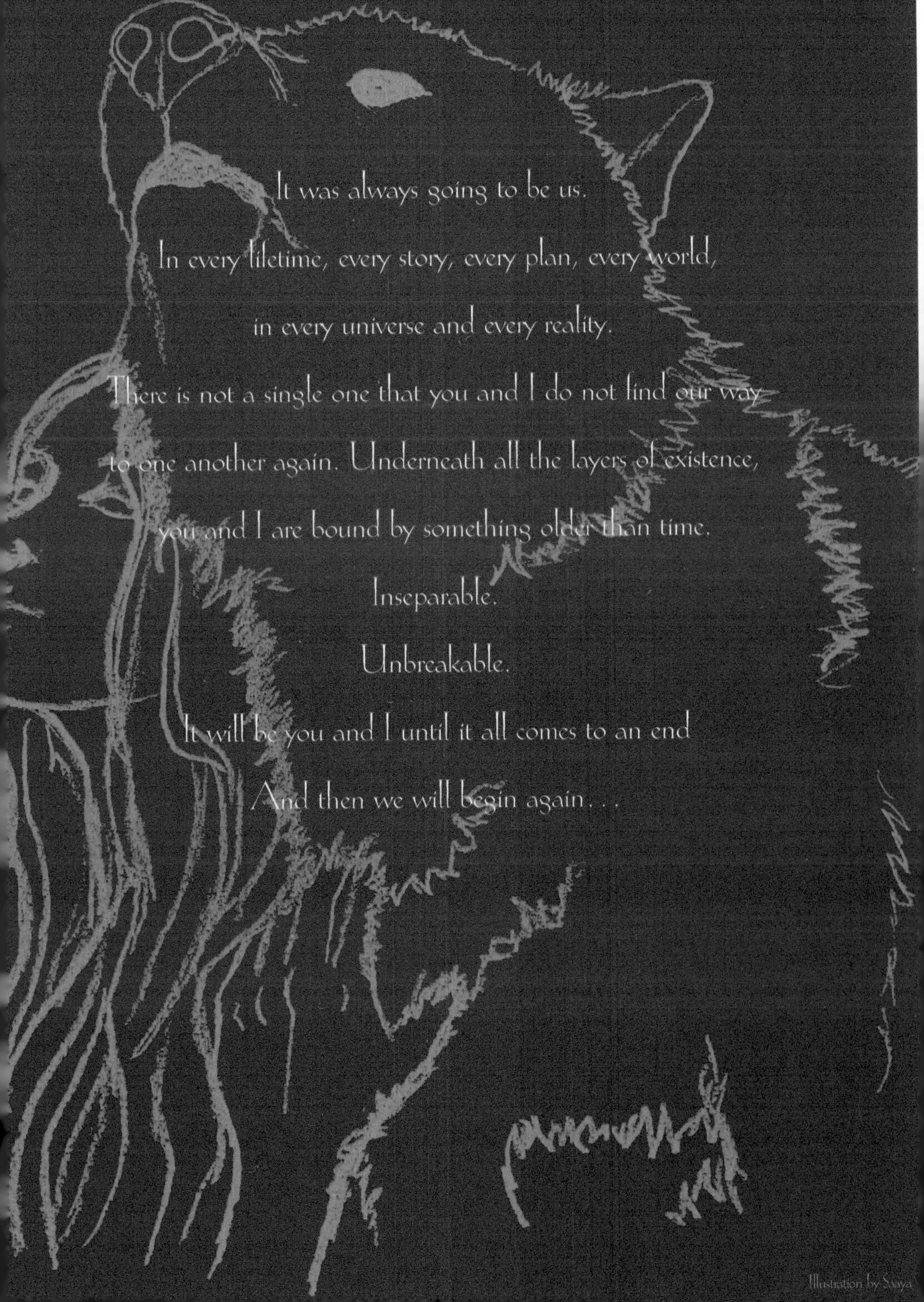

It was always going to be us.

In every lifetime, every story, every plan, every world,

in every universe and every reality.

There is not a single one that you and I do not find our way

to one another again. Underneath all the layers of existence,

you and I are bound by something older than time.

Inseparable.

Unbreakable.

It will be you and I until it all comes to an end

And then we will begin again . . .

Illustration by Saya

WE BELONGED TO EACH OTHER
AN ETERNAL ENTANGLEMENT THAT NOT EVEN DEATH COULD UNDO

I always knew what kind of woman I wanted to be. I spent my adolescence chasing her, nipping at the heels of Wild Woman like a playful and unruly pup, only ever touching the edges of her presence. She planted gardens of wild remedies deep inside my spirit as I played amongst her many shadows. While in the conscious world I suffered. Constantly condensed and reduced to less than all that I was. Told I was too expressive, too free, and wrong in my authenticity.

I was to be seen not heard, I was a body that belonged to the desires and wills of men, I was to be obedient, subservient to make space for a man to "feel like a man" because my muchness was hurting his ego.

It was my fault. My very essence manipulated and abused by the wounds of this world, beating me back into a box that made others more comfortable. Pain seeding deep roots of fear around my heart. I became afraid. I was never truly afraid of the dark, what I feared was what the light might reveal hiding there. What wounds I would find. Walking in the footsteps of who I was to become meant facing the creatures lurking in the place of my fears. The coming of age story.

Where men have been told to take on great quests of heroism and becoming, we children of wolves and women must dive into the underworld and begin the unbecoming.

The unraveling of the lies weaved around who we're told to be, and the descent into our truest and deepest selves. I ran and I chased after this woman I wanted to be until I found myself in a forest dark. Nothing but my skin and the ache in my bones. It was then that they appeared. The first ones to learn and walk the way of the shadows. I asked for their help, but only silence followed. I spent years in their forests, watching, waiting for some message that would bring clarity to my wanderings, and the aching I could not ease. It was in their silence that I learned my fears, my pain, and solitude were a gift. That in the place beyond the false light and masks of the world, I could be raw, real, and free in all that I was. I was taught to dance with the seasons, to play, to sing and howl with the tides of my emotions. I learned that there is wisdom in the wait...

In self-preservation and understanding when to stand my ground and when to fight another day. On the eve of the end of my 9 year, I offered up this unlearning. My shed skin of all that was never truly mine, and I was reborn out of the fires of Wyeast. When I arose from the ashes, the first ones came again. They had long waited for the day when they too would rise again. When all I had learned, and the knowledge forged in my veins would be embodied and given back to the others.

No longer would I chase after this Woman, for when I looked beyond the veil of illusion, I saw her presence within. The woman I wanted to be, was who I always was underneath every lie, restriction, and cage.

No more would I bow, no more would I shrink, no more would I fear my own presence. And no more would I let the kin of the first ones remain in the shadows to be forgotten.

The reason some of us aren't sure who we are when all is
stripped away, is because we are the changeling children.
The mirrors, shifters, tricksters, and mischief makers. We are
here to crack it all open.
With no one true, fixed form,
we call what is known to question.
Bringing forth the forgotten shadows of our kind.
Potential in all its aspects that have been left to the dark.

I am she but in the way of Sidhe.

I am her but as shapeshifter.

They are my ancestors and if you know Them, you know what I mean.

Approach me with the same caution, with kindness, and perhaps I will help

you on your quest.

Come with disrespect and all you touch will turn to ash, luck will never find

you, or shall you be haunted for a lifetime.

I have many voices, many faces, many bodies

To ask me to be just one, is to ask chaos to become order

I am not here to conform, to be digestible, favored, or accepted

I am simply here to be

To leave the faintest trail upon the mossy ground,

to be a whisper of truth,

an echo that others may find so that they too

might be just as they are

You cannot hold a storm in your hands or tame fire without the

risk of dowsing its warmth.

You cannot put wind in a cage. That is who, what they are.

So how do you love them?

You dance in their rain, add kindling and wood to the fire, and

rejoice in the cool breeze as they blow in from their last embarked

journey.

We do not judge these elements for all that they are. Neither too

should we judge a changeling creature in human skin for the way

they exist in our world.

The biggest lie they ever told us was that men see women as weak. The constant effort on their part to create a narrative of weakness in all that is feminine or woman, is the most exposing evidence of the truth. They have always feared what they could not tame or control. Fear is only present in the face of perceived danger or great power. The more intelligent, capable, effective a creature, the greater the effort to minimize the perceived threat. Women are a pure, raw, and unbound force of nature. Capable of bringing life through a portal in our bodies, to physical form on earth. Women can carry the weight of the world's sorrow on their shoulders while continuing to care for others. Our worlds do not stop when we are in pain or suffering. Within a woman lies an infinite wellspring of compassion, and a natural wolf-like instinct that has served to protect not only ourselves, but our loved ones through all of time. The link between wolf and woman, and the fate they have shared at the hands of men, are undeniable. Watch how quickly a weak man reacts to these words. The intensity of the aggressive, dismissive, or defensive way they react to the truth of their history. A man does not try to degrade, shame, destroy, or control a butterfly, a flower, things he does not fear. Only in the face of true power do we witness what it means to be weak.

Weakness is a lack of responsibility for one's self. Reacting without conscious introspection and presence. To speak over, to deny, to fail to listen and be silent. There is a reason why males of the animal kingdom do not survive if they do not find a mate, yet the females of each species continue to carry on. Why it is almost always the males that must dance, court, impress, be the brightest in color, and woo the female in order to pass on his lineage. And why most wild males of any species do not dare press past a rejection or threaten a mother. If all of nature can understand and respect all that is she, it is long overdue that men remember the same. Understand that the way you see us does not define what we are in this world. But it speaks to either your strength or your weakness.

Look to your women.

Look to the wolves.

She appeared upright and just as any other woman to the daylight eyes of those who passed her by. But if your luck fared well, a glimpse of her shadow could be stolen in the sun reigned hours, and you would see not the figure of a woman. Her dark reflection walked on four paws like a phantom wolf silently following behind her. It seems a sacred guardian of her wildish spirit. She was a wolf woman born of darkness and suffering who lived among the beasts of the inner human in solitude. Wandering in the realm of those familiar spirits cast away and abandoned. She sang breath into the unseen, summoning forth an ancient truth from the bones of the forgotten. She howls out in the night stirring deep longing in the hearts of those craving the very essence of being. Roaming mountains of immeasurable height and treachery for pleasure, and swimming in the darkest depths of the void to guide the lost back home. She is the keeper of the eternal flame inside us all. The shadows cast by its illumination are her oldest friends and she dances in the wake of their secrets.

She is the Shadowalker.

# Blessed Samhain/Álfablót


"Thrice burned, thrice reborn"

In honor of Gullveig, the original burned "witch" and first practitioner of Seiðr. As well as honoring every woman and wolf in history who was burned, tortured, and killed for their medicine and magic.

Today is for remembering all who came before us.

For us this is not Halloween, the christianized, colonized mockery and attempted erasure of our history for profit. Today is sacred.

And the blood does not forget.

May the keepers shed the masks they carry in the day and walk unhidden amongst the ancestors tonight. As the rest of the world dresses up in hiding from the spirits, may the walkers peel off their tired disguises to better be found by those who are known to them. Celebrating loved ones passed and welcoming in the coming winter, the dark half of the year where we settle deeply into the bones for rest, reflection, and regeneration.

Artwork by Ludvig Levin

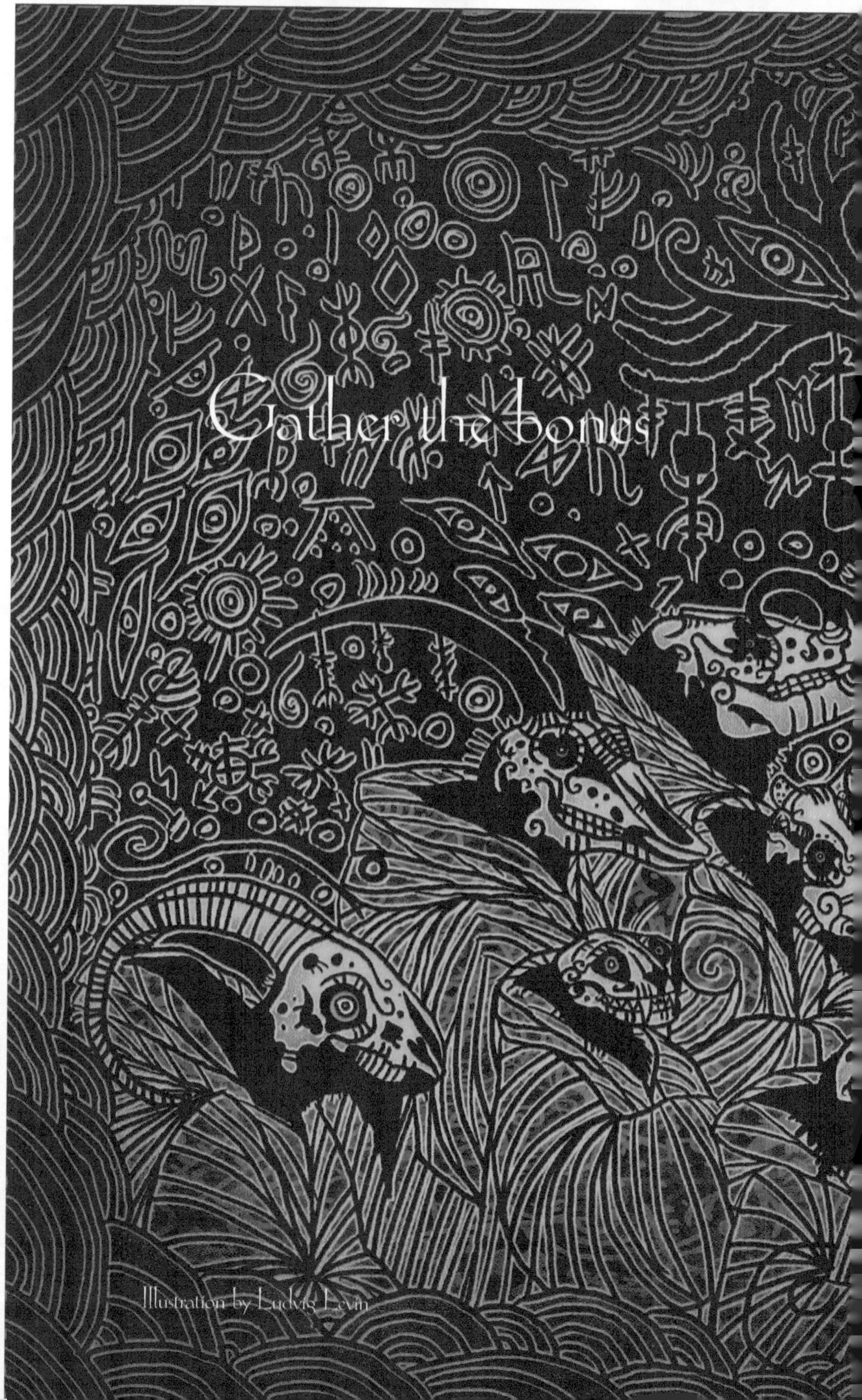
Gather the bones
Illustration by Ludvig Levin

Honor thy dead

I'M ALL THAT'S LEFT

THE REMNANTS OF A DYING WORLD UNKNOWN TO US

WALKING MYTHS OF MEMORIES LONG PAST

I AM THE LORE OF A MILLENNIUM OLD LINEAGE

I AM WHAT'S LEFT BEHIND

AND WHEN I AM GONE

SO TOO WILL THE STORY

When a soul leaves your world, the black wolf comes to see them through
to the otherside.

Their light does not fade in the passage of time as their body does. Your
loved ones join the many glittering lights dancing among the twilight
woods. They sparkle across the night sky, ever lighting your way through
the dark. And for a time, they get to live among the good folk, fluttering
about the edges of your life like hummingbird wings on the summer breeze,
or dew drops on rose petals. The wolves guide their souls, where they can
be with you evermore in the breathing world about you. Next time you
glimpse a flicker in the woods, a shadow passing in the corner of your eye,
a shimmer in the sea,
know that the love of your dear ones is near.
They are with you always…

Artwork by Jade Merien

In our modern age where
most, if not all, of our stories
have been muddled in one
way or another, I choose to
tell these stories the way
they are whispered to me
between dreamings.

I choose to believe faeries and

other kin are a friend to beasts

and dragons.

I hope when it is my time to cross

over, to join the ancestors, that it

is the black wolf I see waiting for

me.

I can hear her; she's closing in ever faster.

There is no escaping once the dark moon rises.

With every push, pull, leap, sprint,

her shadow creeps further upon the ground.

The rattle of bones now deafening,

it commands all other sound into silence.

She has allowed us to flitter about her presence and linger long enough.

The Bone woman has come,

and the time to once again die into the dark is upon us. . . .

May we all honor and remember that we are more than just this body, just this moment. We carry in our blood thousands of generations before us and their collective gifts and wisdom.

It is magic to be here.

To be now.

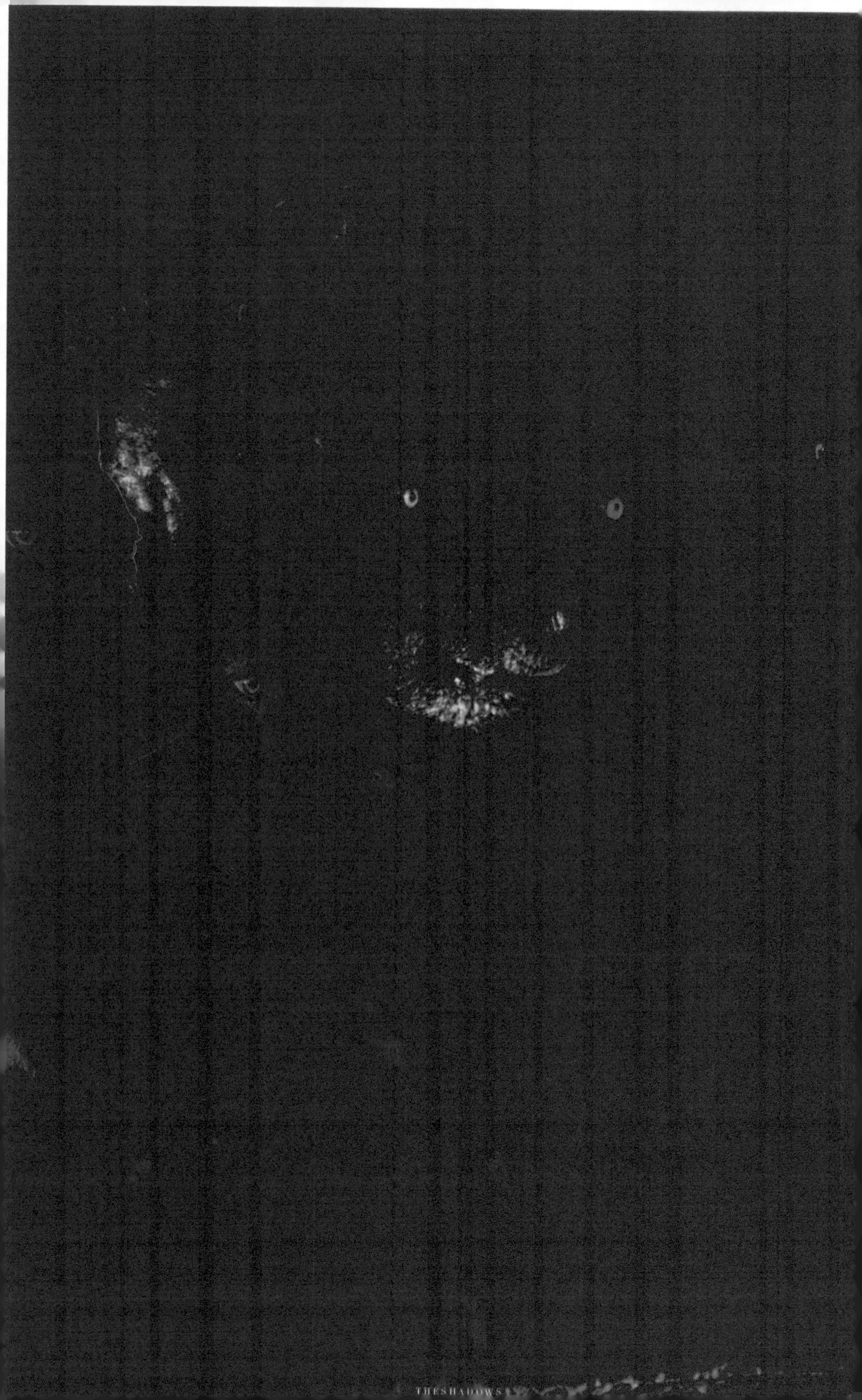
THE SHADOWS

I feel the pull.

Back to the dirt, to the center of life,

to my blood.

Ancestors' and spirits appear more frequently in animal shapes and

dreams.

I used to think "where were you when I was lost?".

In the wake of the storm comes truth. In every stroke of luck or

dodged tragedy. Every time the wind blew my way with a

message. When intuition flared in just the right moment. They

were there. They've been here all along.

I am their living saga, I am their freedom, their dreams, the choices

they didn't have or get to make,

pathways they didn't get to take.

My choices are the act of rebellion that might have ended their lives

and perhaps did.

My heartbeat whispers 'Your life is your ancestor's greatest

treasure. Remember, even in the darkest of nights,

you are never alone'.

I know now why I could never find you.

The teachers, ancestors I felt so far from. Numb too.

I was looking for you in human faces with human voices, all while

feeling that you would likely not come to me this way.

My blood, my support, my wisdoms and lessons, it is in animal kin,

in element, in biome that you reveal your secrets to me.

It is in bubbling of liquid life, the warm blood of mammal, the

languid motion of reptile, whispers feather light on the autumn

breeze.

I was never far from you, nor you from me.

I was never alone or cut away from your gentle hands.

I needed only to stop looking for you where you could not be,

to see you all around me.

Artwork by Martith.

# Spákona and the Great Wolf

Could it be the Great Wolf knew how his story would end? But that from his ending a new world could begin? The Völva with her prophecy and Fenrir with his defeat of Odin ushered in a world no longer ruled by gods. Life began anew.

So often in lore, fairy tales, and myths wolves are portrayed as villains or evil. This has caused fear and hatred to be ingrained in the psyche as it is passed down through the generations. I grew up with these stories as well, though they never quite sat right. Sometimes it is how you interpret the story that changes everything. I have never seen Fenrir and his offspring as the villains. They were victims of hubris, ego, and arrogance. A god king threatened by the reality of mortality seeking to end what he could not control. We see this among many humans, especially in men today. Destroy what will not submit or cannot be controlled. Destroy what we fail to understand. Glorify the man who conquers the beast. But the beasts of these stories have far more to teach us than any of the so-called heroes. This story tells of truth that animal kin feel a vast array of emotions and they remember the sting of betrayal. That like us, they will fight to survive when their lives are threatened. Perspective changes everything. Perspective changes ignorance to understanding. Let's not let the end of wolves be what ushers in a new world of understanding here in our lifetime. We need them now; we need them always.

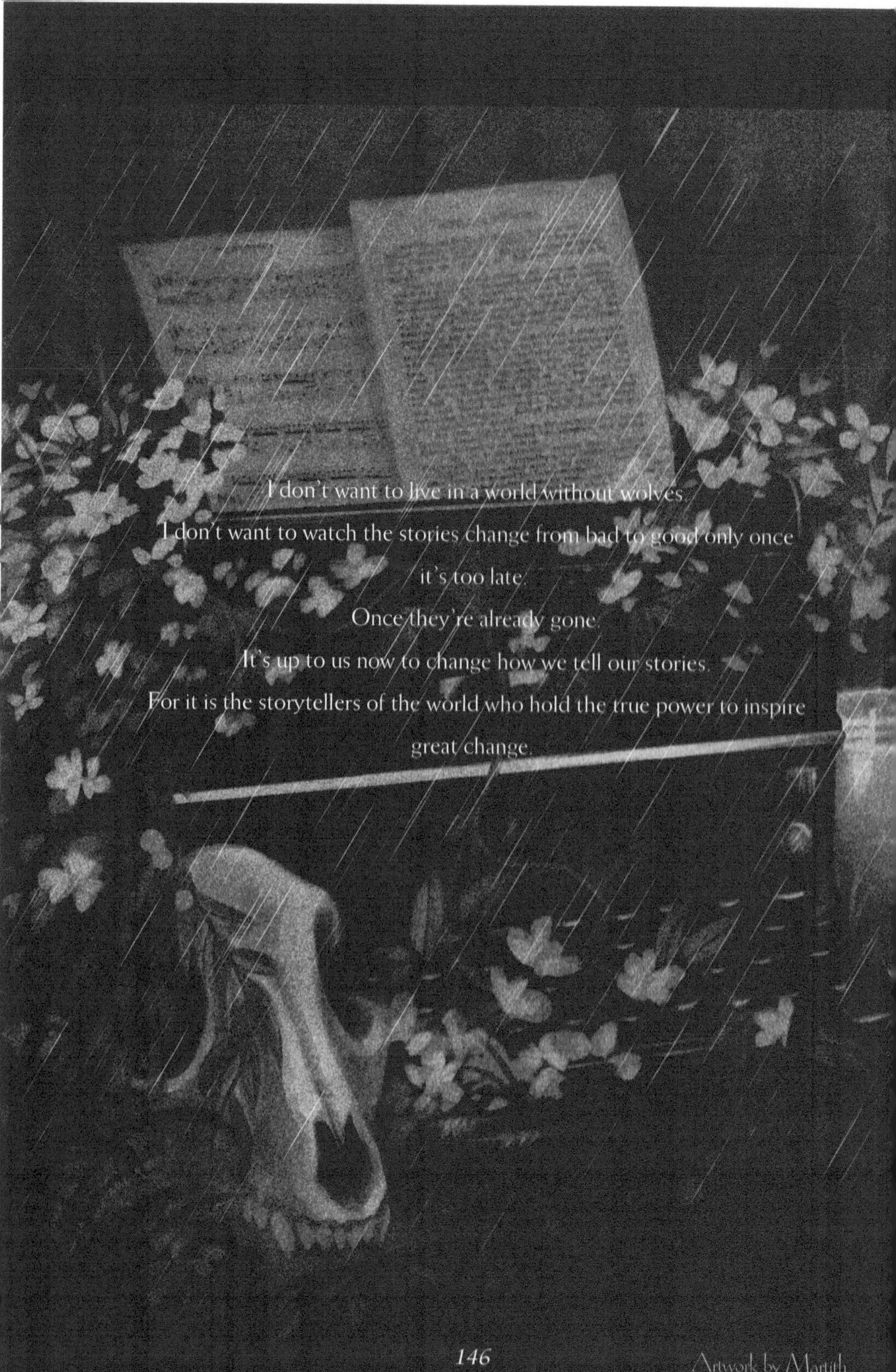

I don't want to live in a world without wolves.

I don't want to watch the stories change from bad to good only once it's too late.

Once they're already gone.

It's up to us now to change how we tell our stories.

For it is the storytellers of the world who hold the true power to inspire great change.

Artwork by Martith

It all makes sense to me now.

What a shadow to face.

The colossal evil of my dysregulated, projected destruction.

Even worse, perhaps it is in there still, only sleeping.

That maybe not much has changed...

But you planted a seed, didn't you?

You were a novice gardener with all the right skills in the worst seasons

of my life. I was the stubborn invasive weed that pricked your fingers

and destroyed your fruits day after day.

Here I am now, in the beginnings of a blooming at last with blood-

stained thorns.

I was the deadly nightshade.

The Wolf's Bane.

But you loved me anyways...

*I would take all of your suffering and swallow it with a smile*

*if it meant you never had to taste this sorrow...*

# GRIEF

The undoing of all that I was and all we could ever be

She grew inside me like thorn covered vines intertwining with my

veins

slowly consuming the landscape of me

Grief was not a force I could outrun

even if I sprouted wings or took to all fours

At the core of my overgrown madness awaited she who held the key

to these sorrowfully locked doors

If only my heart did not quicken with fear

The moment she moved closer

extended hand drawing near

Time,

this thing we say is simply imagined,

feels awfully and

wildly real, uncontrollable.

I feel it quickly slip

through my

fingers like water.

Faster than I can

catch it.

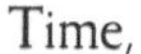

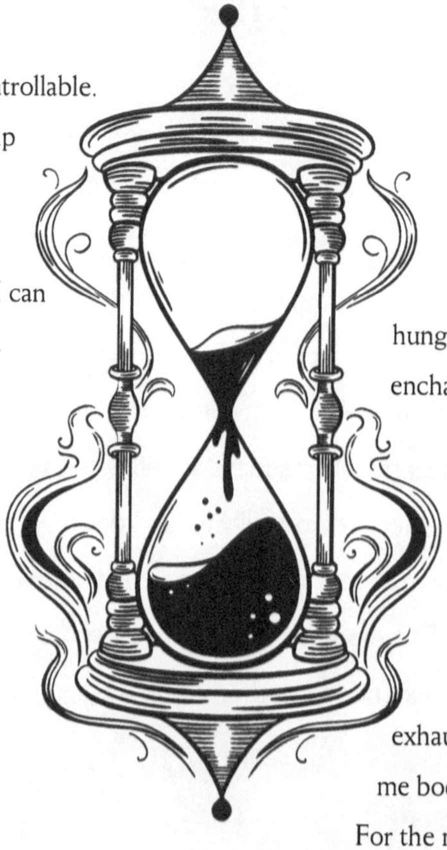

I feel as though a

hungry wolf ever chasing the

enchanted stag, but never to

reach it.

Or if I am at last

to close in

and

quench this

thirst,

exhaustion claims

me body and soul.

For the moment I'm

finally able to seize it in my jaws,

I let it go free. And the cycle goes

on.

The time before feels like another life already...some days I forget that was my life at all. Some days the grief swallows me whole. Maybe that was another place, a story that has died. Maybe those moments are words across burning pages, soon to be nothing but ash. A cremation ground where only scorch marks remain. No bodies, no tombstone, just ghosts. And soon even the marks will fade, but the scar inside will remain.

They say the endless ache is evidence of how much they
meant to you. They say to go on after loss is to keep
loving them and remember them. I remember you often
and the misery is my proof that you were real. That all of
my happiest childhood memories have you in them.
Sometimes the grief of losing you moves all the waters of
the world to fall from my eyes and I swear I'll drown in
it. Sometimes the illusion of linear moments collapse and
dissolve into one another, and I am standing in both my
kitchen, and your doorway at once where you're a
breath away. What is a day without sunlight, without the
warmth of your bear hugs?
But what would I be to give up now, as some of the best
parts of me are shaped by your memory.

For the Tinkerbell to my Pan,

your laugh was the pixie dust to Never Neverland

I said I do believe in faeries with all my heart

but it wasn't enough to keep death from tearing us apart

Now you're the second star to the right

I look for in the morning

To remind me I can fly,

and that life comes without a warning

Would you believe me if I told you I've done all the things we said we'd do

Some of those olden dreams and some of them new

Been a robinhood pirate and given to those in need

befriended dragons, lived with wolves,

and been to worlds we've never seen

All this to say I do believe in faeries

I do I do

And I'll keep your magic with me until all our dreams have come true

As author, allow me to be your vessel and tell your story Mournful One.

Let me tell them how a fledgling carrying a whirlpool of anguish at first frightened by your name, chooses to invite you to sit beside them. They ask softly if you will stay while entering the void of sorrow that threatens to swallow them whole. Let me tell them how because of your welcomed presence, this one did not drown, for you held their hand through the turbulent waters of their pain. And in the moment of surrender; the torment began to subside. You left with the promise you would return the next time you were needed, whether called upon, or time had too long passed.

Thank you spirit of grief, for being a friend. For being a warning that holding on too tightly and denying ourselves our lamenting is slowly killing us. I will tell them your truth, so others too may invite you as friend to sit with their sorrow.

The weight of being glue

What is the opposite of loneliness?

When the time between people coming and going is so evenly

lain that one never has a moments respite to oneself.

I warned myself it would end too soon

and it did…

How many of us carry the weight of holding others together only

to be forgotten?

No one remembers the thread and glue that holds the book

together.

The binding agents go on lost to eternity, never to be known, or

appreciated for their offering and sacrifice.

Yet the book remains, and the story gets told.

Thank you those who have been the glue.

As eldest sister I would take on the gods for the little ones. But who would take on the gods for me? We are the lonely island sibling, the safe haven the others escape too. But we are not supported. We house a dormant volcano ever building pressure beneath the surface of our lives. The crushing weight of the emotional, generational tides ripping at our shorelines. Yet we push up abundant greens and clear waters for those after to have safety, paradise we never had, for as long as we can keep the sleeping volcanic beast at rest. The problem with being this eldest island is eventually, the rage will crack the surface. All that lies beneath will burst through and our little ones will either

be burnt by truth or they will cast off to other lands and we are left even more alone.

Perhaps one day all the scorched earth islands that are eldest siblings will float into one another, creating a land system that supports and nourishes each other. And we will finally be safe to emerge and play in the lush forests we once built for them, together.

They never tell you how the light faded from
their eyes

Or how their heart slowly died

They only talk about how cold and distant they
are

But never the why...

Those who hold so dearly to the priest written telling of the spring maidens' story, have no knowledge of what it is to be snuffed out by the one who birthed them. So controlled and stripped of all autonomy, their flame smothered to smoke they choke on, leaving them silent where screams for freedom would have been. They have no idea how hopeless, powerless it all feels. The cold iron bars of fear from being raised under the tyranny of a narcissus. They couldn't possibly understand what a chance at freedom and devotion would mean to one such as this. What awakening the power within the seemingly powerless would feel like.

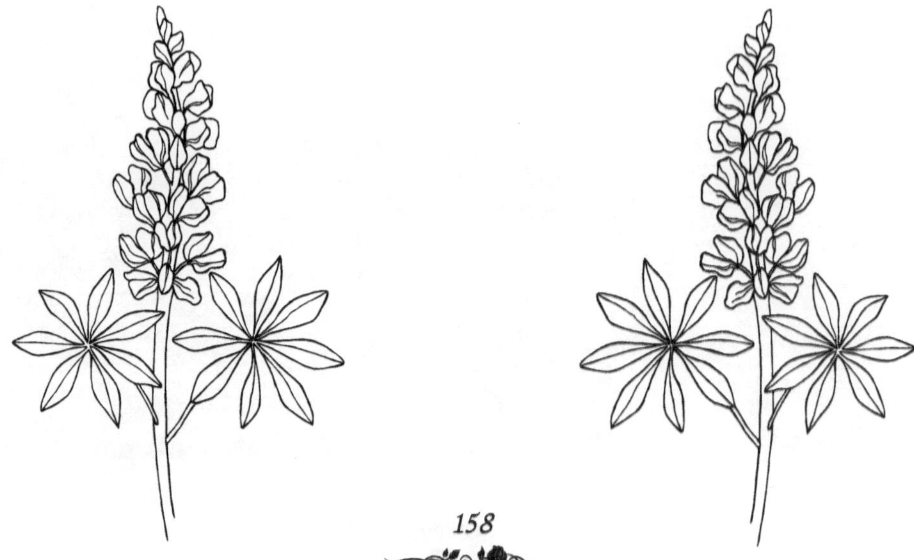

In my womb lives a bramble bush

It grows on everything with thorny vines that coil tight, carve, and scar soft

tissue

Just like a bramble to a lamb, the more I try to free myself, the tighter they

wind

Ever growing roots entwining through flesh and marrow

I bleed within and it brings me to my knees

Consumed by agony with no end,

I'm crushed under osmium fatigue

Another cycle comes to pass, and the blood has run sour….

What was once rich garnet tides has become searing strains of vermillion

and crimson fire

Eruptive blasts send seismic quakes through body and bone

The blood has gone sour,

as vision blurs and I am stripped bare

Pain is all that remains

To see nothing

To hear nothing

There is not but a thousand bolts of lightning ripping through sinew

While the torturous storm ensues, the only sound is strangled cries

pleading for respite that won't come anytime soon

This poisonous, festering sickness took my grandmother from this world

And as I sit frozen in terror, heart irregular and erratic,

with death coursing through shallow veins,

I hope it will not take me too…

Do you know how it feels to be infinitely expanding,

full and filling still,

but trapped in tight wrapping,

constricting more at every attempt to free yourself?

And then to be forced within iron bars called

purpose, work, worth?

Has it ever felt like your bones would break themselves to pieces

just to escape?

The tremors so violent,

you fear any moment your body could choose to end it.

But to fight it, is to try to stuff a tsunami back into the sea.

It will only grow in strength and fury until your ribs can

no longer hold it at bay.

Artistry dances behind heavy lids

But a dam keeps me from the spring

I'm trapped again in titanium bars of fatigue and shame

Cringe, weird, freak, unwell, unstable, defective, dangerous

I'm

dangerous?

And my nails elongate sinking into the umber earth

Bones twist and break beneath my skin and I hold every breath to keep from

screaming

The salt of my sweat burns like acid

But still I keep it all in

Keep it all together

No one can see that I'm nearly catatonic

That's what they call it right?

But I am not unwell, I am in pain

You try holding a hurricane within your frame and tell me what it does to you

If only I could open my eyes and see the bars aren't real

Artwork by Ziva Ivadottir

Listen, and the nothing will speak…

I was never meant to feel 'right' in my own shape as some might.

That is the fate of the shiftlings.

All my life I wanted to know who I was, what I was, where do I fit in the cosmic scheme.

It seems it is in the non-belonging, in the unanswered, the reason unveils itself.

I was not meant to know, to pick one course, to master.

To feel comfortable in this form would mean becoming a falsified fragment of what I could be.

I'm not special, not chosen,

I want to unsettle you with my existence so that you can free yourself by asking why.

Outcast of society, outlier of the systems, that is the next step in our evolution.

We cannot change what we comply with, what we adapt to accept.

'What is' may only be changed by transforming beyond the place we are now.

What they say makes you uncomfortable

The way they speak

The way she looks

The way his shoulders aren't broad enough

The way my eyes look through your bullshit and see the truth that is inside

Why would anyone listen

Why would anyone like us

When society has made it so damn easy to just swipe past us

Block, censor, delete

Algorithms to support the dopamine addiction

Another hit of cortisol for the keyboard warriors who are really drowning

in self-loathing, crying for help because these cities have taken place of

forests, and the monsters we fight now are dressed as saints we look up to

Another hit

Another dollar

Another hour of overtime

Another binge sesh with our friend Flix

And the brain rot goes on and on

You're lost in the madness and time is running out

The only way out is through

And we're coming for you

Discomfort is the doorway and the void is calling

One look in the mirror and you know you want it

You're tired of being tired and misery no longer needs your company

It's time for the one on one

Suddenly everyone wanted to be a friend after
we clawed our way out of the Filth and muck.
The same ones who couldn't be bothered with
our suffering and the struggle of our strange
ways of being, now sent pleasantries or bowed
heads with false attempts at reentry.
Of course, access is wanted when one's fragility
is replaced with power. When our humanness is
less visible and instead mystery surrounding us
in intrigue takes its place.

Like glass you thought I would shatter,

but these bruises are proof that I am made of dark matter,

and when under pressure,

I will burst into galaxies.

You cannot break the infinite expanse of space.

Too big for your boundaries, bodies, or borders.

I am the voice in the void.

Chaos and noise.

The black hole that will swallow all light and darkness and give birth to

beauty untamed.

We say no,

we will not make infamous the thing that was done and give legacy to that evil.

For the ones who commit such acts hold no remorse or regret.

We will not allow them to take up space in our art, our stories, our creativity.

Our journeys and who we are is of no credit to them.

We were already strong, already forged with courage and

magic and steel..

They did not bring it out in us.

We rose from the ashes of the fire they thought would leave us in ruin, and they

will forever be the unwritten,

and unforgiven.

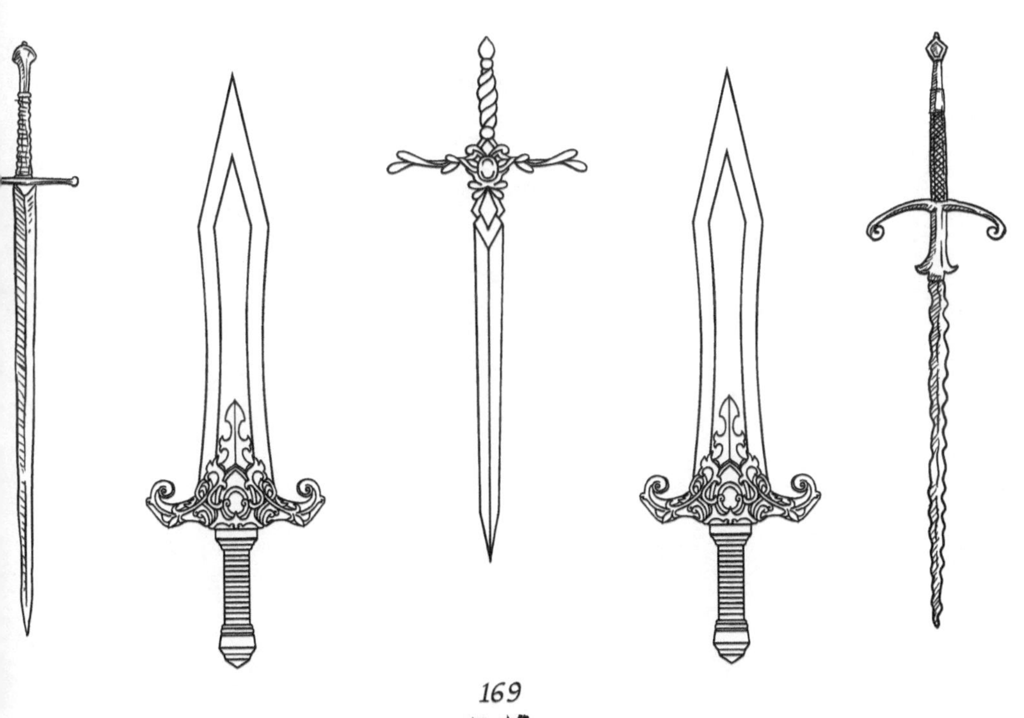

The destruction I could bring if I unsheathed the sword
behind my teeth. I could sink fangs into flesh and tear
all that bravado from your chest.
But I wouldn't sully my mouth with the poison in your
veins.
I prefer to let the plague of my silence, my absence
eat away at your mind, slowly driving you insane.
Words will run your throat dry, and you'll choke on
arrogance's thick smoke. Rage is sacred, hatred— a
wounded soldier that awaits wrath to take their place.
Anger is a holy emotion.
A gift.
One you will never receive,
as I owe you no part of me.

If I was that easy to kill, I'd be dead already

And yet I remain

I crawl, I limp, I bend and break, and yet still I stand

I will gnaw off my own paw before I let you be the end of me

Lightning strikes a deep cerulean sky

An ancient tree growing from my shoulder to my eye

The wheel stops turning, and I tear it from its mount

There will be no legacy, no memory or tale to recount

It ends with me

The storybook closed

You die with me

Thorn of a rose

They have no authority in the sacred space of me.

Nor do they have right to feel pride in me,

for I am of myself,

of my comrades,

forged family,

and the wild kin that all hold me.

I am neither a product of their creation, nor solely of my own.

I am spirit and ancestor made,

rain and storm watered,

fauna and flora fed,

mountain and sea supported.

I was raised by the voices that whisper between heartbeats and

resound through the core of a dying star.

I remember the very moment when enough was enough. When the

endless pleading and screams fell silent. When I took fate back into my

own hands.

I left the scorching unholy light of the "gods" behind and returned to the

dark,

the shadow, the deep womb that was the wellspring.

At the mouth of the bone cave, I stood and wondered if I would be

welcomed home or swallowed whole.

Into the underground sea of memory, I went and drifted into the shades

of myself and those who came before me. The husk of the old way of

being was cracking all around me, and I sang for the birth of a new oath,

emerging, convulsing, erupting just beneath the surface.

The words were mine and not mine, but the resonance in my throat was

burning with scorching truths and

rebellious revelations.

Depression has come for another visit.

Colors and sound either diluted or adding to the madness. I envy those with normal energy and drive to function. Some days the heavy grabs me and takes me under the dark tides with no warning.

I miss the deep forest, the mist, the permeating silence atop the slumbering snow peaked mount. Where I breathe for the first time and my lungs burn with life, instead of fear.

My bones ache in sweet symphony of living.

It seems as though all other times I am animated involuntarily. A necromancer keeping me from peaceful repose. But in those sacred spaces between, my lungs bloom with greenery and I am not simply reanimated,

I am reborn.

My wolf skin, my raven wings, the oceanic waters of my body stirring life anew, summoning me from the depths, from deep-rest.

Next time you are called sensitive, remind them
you carry the sorrow of those who walked before you.
Their rage, their guilt, their unfulfilled wishes.
You are the point where rivers flow into the sea.
A melding of so many lives.

We are never truly alone, no matter how it seems at the time.

There is someone else who understands, and

someone else who is glad you are here. There are others wishing they

had someone like you in their lives. We can't possibly know the entirety

of what we mean to other people. But when we brave the choice to

believe we matter, and to reach back into the dark for one another, we

find what is worth living for.

Take care of yourselves,

Take care of each other

A different kind of warrior

One who's sword and shield are in the beating of their heart and the draw of their breath when everything screams for them to cease. It is in the rise of their body after being kicked to the filth over and over again.

Their armor is in the love of those who care for them.

And their legacy in the kindness they continue to extend out into the world, no matter the cruelty they've seen.

Some warriors don't go to a physical war.

Sometimes the battle wages inside their mind and body, and the scars tear at the soul. These are the unseen heroes. And the most needed ones in our world.

I see you

I shall walk beside you in the shadows and be the echo in the void that softly whispers, "you are not alone'.

You are not unseen by me.

I will be the gentle breeze that kisses your scars as a reminder that even the darkest parts of ourselves deserve gentleness and love.

Photograph taken by Rachel Lauren

What need have I of the gods when it was the darkness itself

who came to my aid

The most ancient force in all existence reached out their loving

hand and held me gently

Gave me refuge

Let me rest, recover,

until I was ready to rise

The other side of the coin is this

Honeyed wine, mortal essence

The body's fall equinox

This gift of release, of cleansing

Rosewood drips down cavern walls

bringing spells of enchanted sleep

Womb folk take on wilder forms and move in bearish nature

Forage, nurture thy body, become great guardian of self

and home

As leaves of scarlet and carmine fall from the great tree

Descent into dark burrows and hibernation begins

The bleed feels like the only time I truly come home to this body

When I have no choice but to bend to her will

To submit, to surrender

My soul jolted back into my flesh and deep into the earth

The one time being human feels sacred

Feels right

The price of a rose is paid in blood

# CARMILLA

Honeyed nectar crimson red

Ðrips down fair lips in passions stead

One taste one touch, the promise said

Forever her lover, thy heartbeat dead

My love is a wild beast roaming the caverns beneath my ribs.

To try to capture it, tame it, is the moment it is lost.

You cannot trap a wild creature and ask it to change shape to love you.

You can befriend it, accept the wild things for what they are, and hold fast

to the moments they choose to stay near. Leave a wild one free and they will

return time and time again. I find there is no greater love than this,

the love of choice. The love that returns for no other

reason than it so wishes to be reunited, to share company and soul once more.

Untamed, unbound, unrestricted love.

Love through the ages, love of a moment.

Her passion was a match in a room full of candles. She does not give her fire away, only ignites flames to burn in others.

You could not help but be stirred and impassioned yourself in the wake of her love.

She walked with a freedom that had the power to break chains just by being near her.

I have no desires to change or tame her.

If she must love you and she must love me,

I love her all the same.

What you share does not take from me,

nor do I take from you.

You are a part of her, as I am,

and I will protect what she cares for.

I love her as a whole,

not merely the pieces that fit to my liking.

It feels as though the parts of me that are afraid are the parts
that remember
The fibers still entwined with that other time
when I lay magma veined with scorched skin
And sulfuric heat rose from between
parted charred lips
When each heartbeat sent an
earth-shattering quake
through the
landscape
of you

I am blissfully, torturously
haunted by the possibilities, by the unknown.
Phantom hands linger, caressing my mind with delicious
agony. They whisper "remember",
but remembrance is only a taste of what is to come.

The dark and golden light both take me as lover.

One spreads slow and warm over naked flesh and feels of blooming.

The other devours and swallows me whole.

I am a creature of this space between dusk and dawn

And the voice in the dark whispered,

'Do not be afraid dear one

It is you who called me here

I would come for no other reason than to serve you

You are safe in my love...'

I always return to the shadow,

and you're always there waiting.

The ache goes on and on...

Once again haunting my dreams with longing as I desperately

cling to the edge of memory.

Any glimpse I can have,

and yet you always slip away without a trace.

Like sand in an hourglass,

I cannot stop the way my mind takes you away.

Only my heart remembers.

How can this feeling be imagined?

Please…

just this once,

stay.

In my eternal short years, I have found the monsters to be the saviors of the stories. The gentle, the merciful, the forgiving. The moment they're shown a kindness and seen for who they are, the moment the illusionary fear slips away, dissipating in a passing breeze.

It is the beast that is the secret treasure.

Holding love, passion, loyalty behind fang and claw sharpened on the lies and harm done by the world. Only meant to protect self from further maiming. It seems to me it is the self-proclaimed heroes, the holy, and full of might that create the broken. How ever could their light shine without a shadowy backdrop? Their victories fall on blind eyes and deaf ears for no one cares what you've done when there is nothing to fear and no one to save. Their might dwindles under the weight of their self-importance unrealized. How noble and heroic are they once their name no longer leaves tongue or cheek and the monsters are all in love?

It is the monsters who passionately devour.

Who hold every piece of us and savor the taste to the very last drop.

As they say, the hero will sacrifice you to rescue an ungrateful world that will forget them soon after they're gone.

It is the villain who will burn all the injustice to the ground for love.

I can take you down to the bone and piece you back

together again.

Tendon by tendon,

sinew and marrow,

cell by cell.

All you need but do is surrender.

The villain and saint go at it again

The dark and light within entangle and the animal is released

Clawing into earth and flesh

Howling

Tearing to bone

A symphony of night song, your scent calls to me and I want to drag

my teeth across your throat

I want to sink in and feel the warmth of your blood as it runs over my

tongue

The essence of living smeared between hungry bodies and gasping

breaths

Feral

Frenzied

Moon scorched

Unhinged and untamed

A creature of wolf and shadow

Your name tastes just as sweet as it leaves my lips, I want to drown in

you slowly

Suck the air from my lungs or else I'll breathe fire

Dig your nails into my skin, and give me the look that

beckons me to devour

# I BET YOUR BONES ARE BEAUTIFUL

My mouth runs dry and tastes of sand,

parched by the absence of reciprocity.

This body a barren land haunted by the spectres of my memory.

I wish for the waters of my soul to flow over my cracked tongue and down my

ravaged throat,

filling my belly with enchantment and songs of desire once more.

Resurrecting the many pleasures of this fruitful youth,

I wish to burst courageously into bloom.

If lovers have left my spirit athirst, it is I who must pour into the cracks in my

skin calling forth evermore.

So that I might yet again flow with healing rapids

and the will to fill another.

Without light, there would be no division into shadow. Only unity within the blackness. Light is what permits us to stand separate from our true selves. From the versions of us we abandon to the dark.

So remember next time you turn to shame those phantoms lurking about the day. The brighter the dawn, the more strength in the shadow.

Boar spirit is calling to me.

Boar's strength, loyalty to their clan, wisdom, persistence,

determination.

The will needed to push through.

To stand and fight for one's place.

Algiz came for a time, they linger still.

But Boar is visitor now.

Requesting presence and attention now.

May I learn from Boar spirit and gain the strength needed to face

challenges and persist courageously.

Existing unapologetically.

Such grief, such anguish to allow our souls to dwindle slowly as
we cast bit by bit to the abyss, filling our minds with distraction and
high after high to escape the truth. We let the societal world
convince us to enact violence on our own being and do the
stripping away for them.
They need not even dirty their hands,
we so willingly offer up our golden rays out of fear of rejection,
exile.
We offer up our gifts,
our power at the cost of our sanity.
It is time to end the extracting.
It is time to descend the dark and reclaim each and every fleck of
stardust that has been left to be shamed and forgotten.
You are not broken.
You are the dormant star waiting to burst and burn.
Follow the portal people. Those supernovas turned blackhole that
are gateways to other glittering worlds.
There you will find all the pieces of you.

To see the intricacies of your soul, I am enmeshed,

you are I, I am you, we are they, a part of this infinite existence. There

are kin lying dormant in every being from our atoms to the mountain

peak, to the ice crystals of Pluto and beyond.

Something must awaken them.

Thus, enters those of whom society would call exile, dangerous, a flaw

in their system.

There have been legends, books, songs, paintings, every kind of

expression of who we are and what we are here for.

You already know too don't you…

the space between each heartbeat has whispered to you this truth.

You are one of us.

There are others out there,

stirring, writhing, cracking open, remembering,

crawling up from the deep underbelly into the here and now.

To walk this earth on ancient feet and defy the empiric colosseums that

have enslaved us all. You see there is no free as you know it. Even those

in power crumble under the weight of losing it, melded as one into the

endless race to obtain more.

In the pursuit of expression we aim for perfection. Edit this, cut that, rewrite this, it could be improved, it can't be saved, and we tear into our authentic creations until the energy and spirit of that which was attempting to come through has been riddled no more than a hollow shell.

In the name of approval.

Who's approval?

This is the mind games arena.

What if for a moment, we allow the energy moving through limbs to finger tips, eyes, throat, lips, feet to be just as it is.

A child born from our soul to be loved, accepted, and allowed to find its way through the world. Perfection is an illusion, the unattainable because it is not real. It is merely a trick of wits.

No one ever told us growing up that being invisible in plain

sight is a superpower. Imagine what you can create, what

you can accomplish if no one's watching?

If no one cares? Free from scrutiny and judgement.

If they're not paying attention, let them.

The chance for raw unbridled creation is yours for the

taking.

Letters to a younger self


Little one, you are capable of more than you can guess right now.

Let me tell you, you are going to fulfill every dream you have, although it may not look quite like you imagine. You will befriend dragons who may not don scales you can fathom. You are going to run with wolves, and rest in the stars. You will learn to speak with animals in forgotten languages beyond the human. You will befriend giants, serpents, and spirits. You will find your family. It won't be marked by blood, but by bonds of trust and choice. You will grow and you will play, you will daydream and pretend. You'll find out why you always felt so different and that there are a lot of others like you too. Those are your people. Never forget how capable, adaptable, and compassionate you are. You are good. There are beautiful things that exist inside you even if you may not always see them. You will impact others in ways you don't yet know, and they will remember you.

You have so many walking beside you,

even if you cannot see or hear them,

keep going.

Rest when you need, love as much as you can,

and never let the world close up your heart.

Someone, somewhere is thanking their gods you exist,

and so am I.

The great
trees
of the forest do
not shame the newly
sprouted spruce.
They do not see the
sapling as any less
of a tree than
they are.

There is true power in authenticity.

Never show up as anything less than all that you are.

Others will always want, extract from, and imitate what they lack in themselves. Don't let it stop you from creating, from saying this is me.

That is your strength.

That is your gift to the world.

209

Photograph by Cyrena Rose

You've been working so tirelessly and trying so hard to
stop those familial patterns in their tracks. Interrupting
their automated response and consciously choosing to
act from your heart.

I see you.

You are brave.

It does matter and you are making a difference.

I am proud of you for continuing even when it's hard.

Even when its uncomfortable. Perfection isn't the goal,
the effort and small changes are, and you're trying.

The Red Woods did not grow to great heights
overnight.

Keep going.

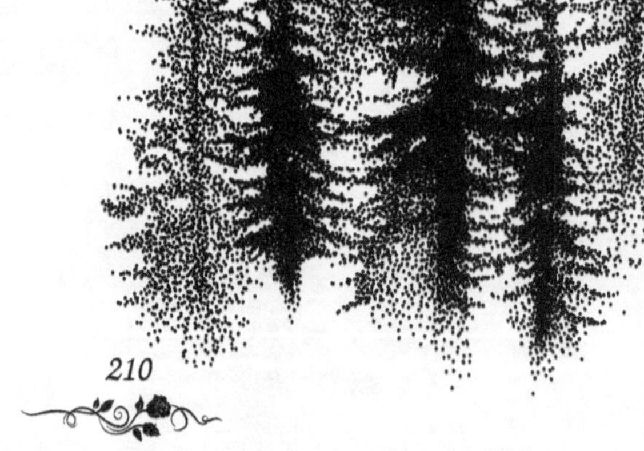

When your mind toils in the constant chatter, your
physical form wrought with exhaust, and your soul is
singed with grief,
Go to the water.
You have always been a ward of the water, and they
call you back when you need to remember.
Water will hold you gently, when you cannot hold
yourself.
Photograph by Cin and Stone

Photograph by Cin and Stone

Let the wild voice guide the way

My words are my tribute and oath to remember and protect the
bond between all of our kinds. The Wolves are my elders, my kin,
our family, and we owe our survival as a species to their wisdom and
their friendship.... This is my promise to not let the world forget.

If you asked me what I am made of,

I would tell you

Of Wolf And Shadow

I CARE NOT IF THE WORLD FORGETS ME OR NEVER KNOWS MY NAME.

IF I AM JUST ANOTHER NAMELESS SHADE BETWEEN THE AGING PAGES OF

OUR HISTORY

ALL I WANT IS FOR THEM TO KNOW AND REMEMBER YOU

TO KNOW YOUR SOUL WAS HERE AND HOW YOU CHANGED SOMEONE'S LIFE

FOREVER

SAAYA, THIS IS FOR YOU


THESE ARE THE BONES OF THE BODY THAT IS TO COME

# AUTHOR'S FINAL MESSAGE

I didn't write this to sound eloquent, or to be a great writer, or to even be remembered. I wrote this to be human. There have always been critics of the arts. And often the critics are those lacking the bravery for vulnerability required to create authentically, so they spend their time judging and picking apart the expressions of others. This book is a mess, my writing and voice are in no way genius or even new. But it is human. Unedited, unaltered by other opinions and rules on what makes it good art or not. I wrote this because even if I fail and look foolish, I hope it inspires someone to do better. It was the bravery of artists that gave me the confidence enough to put my own creative works out into the world. I hope my writing does the same for someone else and they put out a piece of themselves truly marvelous. I hope every person who hates my writing and thinks they can do better, does just that. I hope they write, and create, and share. I do not care if critics think this book is garbage. I'm proud of myself garbage. There is a little me watching with joy filled tears in her eyes that I was brave for us both.

So go forth and do the scary thing!

Create in whatever way calls to your soul.

It is the one thing we are truly meant to do.

# The Wolves of: Of Wolf And Shadow

Within these pages you were introduced to a few of the special wolves and wolfdogs that have shaped my journey. I have met, photographed, worked with, helped rescue/rehome/train, and befriended over 100 wolves and wolfdogs in the last 11 years. So many of them have taught me invaluable lessons, helped shape who I am now and continue to guide me in who I am still becoming. I could probably write an entire book about them, but I hope for now, this little tome will do. A special thank you to Justice and Sadie. The wolf who found me, and the one who ignited the flame. To Lucian and Rachel, my first mentors and now dear friends. To Kato, Nakita, Nymeria and Ashley for bringing the best person I've ever been honored to know into this world and trusting me to be his companion. With all the gratitude and love and appreciation in my heart, thank you with all I have to Saaya and Ekko. I would not be here without them.

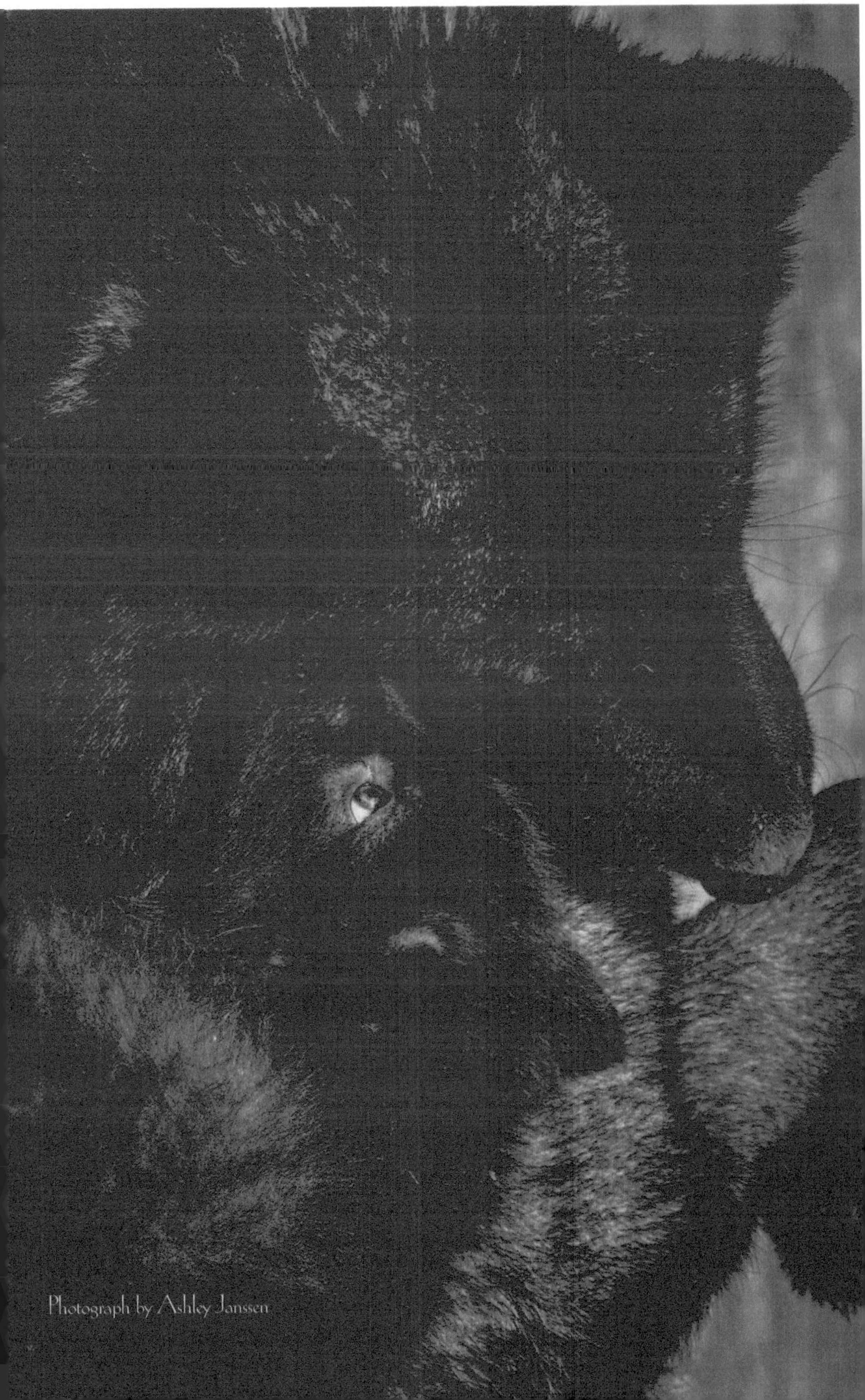
Photograph by Ashley Janssen

# ARTIST ACKNOWLEDGEMENTS


Cover Art: Sofie Draheim, United Kingdom

Instagram: @Draugaskald

TikTok: @Draugaskald

www.draugaskald.com/

Cover border art, interior cover spread, back interior

cover spread, back cover, page

52,53,70,71,73,94,121,214 Art:

Sarah Fastenmeier, Germany

Instagram: @Luriusa

Twitter: @Luriusa

Page 93 Art: HesterAspland, Scotland

Instragram: @hesteraspland

www.hesterasplandillustration.co.uk

with printed permission by Warhorns Festival UK

Page 58,100,101,131-133,180,181,199 Art:

Ludvig Levin, Sweden

Instragram: @the.oak.arts

Page 103 Art: Shannon Cornell, Norway

Instagram: @elvenwolves

Tiktok: @Elvenwolves

Twitter: Elvenwolves_

Page 31,104,135,143,146,Art: Martith, Chile

Instagran: @martith.art

Website: http://martith.art

Page 163 Art: Ziva Ivadóttir , Iceland

Instagram: @strigaartist

FB: Striga Artist

www.striga.is

Page 136 Art: Jade Merien

Instagram: @jademerien

Page 51,97,179 Photography:

Rachel Lauren Robertson, OH

Instagram: @ohiocanidcenter

www.ohiocanidcenter.com

Page 21 Art: Jade/ Kaaena

Instargram: @kaaena_

Wolfdogs drawn are Ravn (blackphase) and Kodiak

(white), Sweden

Instagram: @wild_lupines

# ARTIST ACKNOWLEDGEMENTS

Page 45, 108, 211,212 Photography:

CinAndStone, PNW

Instagram: @cinandstone

Page 66 & 209 Photography: Cyrena Rose, CA

Instagram: @cyrenarosecreative

Facebook: Cyrena Rose Photography

Page 44 & 219 Photography: Ashley Janssen, PNW

Instagram: @northwestwolfdogs

Page 4,17,67,105,171 photography and

14,18,20,24,37,63,106,117,118,123,129,201,213

doodles:

Of Wolf And Shadow

All socials: @ofwolfandshadow

First Illustration of Saaya: Meraea Hennessey

Instagram: @hennessygathering

Page 99 Art: Bex Dartnall. Czech Republic

Instagram: @gyldafyr

Etsy: Gyldafyr

Page 53 Art: Keri Duckworth

Instagram: @wildkeri

Page 64 Art Freedom: Harley Volf

Instagram: @harleyvolf

OfWolfAndShadow is so much more than this book.

For all of time humans have made art and told stories. stories hold the power to shape our world. religion, history, scientific research, music, movies, paintings, etc are all forms of storytelling that greatly impact our beliefs about the world around us. it is my goal to use as many forms of creative expression and storytelling as i can alongside my canine companions to help shift the narrative for all of us outcasts, especially for wolves.

If you'd like to learn more you can find us at

OfWolfAndShadow on all socials

and

ofwolfandshadow.com

# SOME READING RECOMMENDATIONS

Women Who Run With The Wolves by Clarissa Pinkola Estes

Braiding Sweetgrass by Robin Wall Kimmerer

Beyond The Human Essay by So and Pinar Sinopoulos-Lloyd featured on

Atmos Earth

Spell of the Sensuous by David Abram

Lost Teachings of the Runes by Ingrid Kincaid

Promise of the Wolves by Dorothy Hearst

Draugaskald by Sofie Draheim

Oaken Tongue by L. Morton

The Wisdom of Wolves by Elli H. Radinger

Trolls by Brian Froud

Pilu in the Woods by Mai K. Nguyen

Waiting for Wolf by Sandra Dieckmann

Wolf Time By Barbara J, Moritsch

Wolf Woman by Sherryl Jordan

Illustration by Sarah Fastenmeier

www.ingramcontent.com/pod-product-compliance
Lightning Source LLC
Chambersburg PA
CBHW032251070726
47590CB00016B/2115

9 781922 936905